MW00786001

The Boston Trustee

To Flip,

with best wishes,

Tom Bett

The Boston Trustee

Thomas E. Bator

Heidi A. Seely

DAVID R. GODINE, *Publisher*

BOSTON

First published in 2015 by
DAVID R. GODINE, *Publisher*
Post Office Box 450
Jaffrey, New Hampshire 03452
www.godine.com

LIBRARY OF CONGRESS CATALOGING-IN-PUBLICATION DATA
Bator, Thomas E. author.
The Boston trustee : the lives, laws, and legacy of a vital institution /
Thomas E. Bator and Heidi A. Seely.
pages cm
Includes bibliographical references and index.
ISBN 978-1-56792-547-0 (alk. paper)
1. Trusts and trustees –Massachusetts. 2. Investment advisors –Legal status,
laws, etc.–Massachusetts. 3. Trusts and trustees–Social aspects–
Massachusetts –Boston. I. Seely, Heidi A. author. II. Title.
KFM2537.B38 2015
346.74405–dc23
2015024994

First edition, 2015
Printed in the United States of America

Acknowledgements

THE FOLLOWING PEOPLE were helpful in reading early drafts of our work and providing comments: Eric P. Hayes, who provided invaluable assistance from the beginning of this project; Scott C. Steward, Harold I. Pratt, and Patricia D. Popov. Pam Bator proofread and helped us find the thread of the story. Professor John H. Langbein's extensive and detailed comments were also invaluable, as were comments by Professor Charles E. Rounds, Jr. The improvements are theirs, while the errors remain ours. Sara Eisenman worked tirelessly to perfect the look of the book and its contents. David Godine was gracious to publish our work.

Tim Knowlton was instrumental in helping us to get the book published, and we are grateful for his help.

The partners of Nichols & Pratt, LLP provided us with the time, patience and space to research and write this work. Thank you.

The following institutions provided valuable assistance, helping us to find and allowing us access to materials for the book: The Boston Athenæum, The Massachusetts Historical Society, The Harvard Law School Library, The Massachusetts Judicial and State Archives, and The City of Boston Archives.

To my four best friends: my wife, Pam, and my children, Alice, Kate and Henry

TEB

To the Boston Trustees who provided me with the opportunity to dive into this fascinating and fulfilling profession

HAS

Contents

Preface

You'll get mixed up, of course,
as you already know.
You'll get mixed up
with many strange birds as you go.
So be sure when you step.
Step with care and great tact
and remember that Life's
a Great Balancing Act.
Just never forget to be dexterous and deft.
And never mix up your right foot with your left.[1]

"WHAT IS A BOSTON TRUSTEE?" I asked. It was the Spring of 1991 and my friend Jack Herbert and I were having lunch. Jack had just told me that he was going to go work for a Boston Trustee named Harry Guild. Like me, Jack was a trusts and estates lawyer at a large Boston law firm. The economics of practicing trusts and estates at a large law firm are difficult. Overhead is high and a pyramid of associates and legal assistants is needed to support the partners, so billing rates and hourly minimums need to be comparably high. The actual practice of trusts and estates law, with its personal service and slower pace, is difficult to execute in such an economic vise. I had grown up in Cambridge, Massachusetts, and had a law professor as a father, but I had never heard of a Boston Trustee. The concept sounded interesting – an individual who, as a profession, acted as a trustee for families.

Later that year, I was invited to lunch by a different Harry, Harold I. Pratt. Harry was a partner in the Boston Trustee office of Nichols & Pratt. After several conversations and interviews, I was hired in January of 1992 by Nichols & Pratt. At the time, I joked to Jack Herbert, who had begun working for "his" Harry, that we would get together in ten years to work together as partners. I eventually became a partner of Nichols & Pratt, and approximately ten years after my prediction, Jack Herbert joined us as a partner.

Since joining Nichols & Pratt, I have become interested in the history of the Boston Trustee, a special subset of individual professional trustees. In 1995, Eric Hayes, my friend with an unequalled and encyclopedic knowledge of trust law, asked me to be the Secretary to his Chairmanship of the committee reviewing the Uniform Prudent Investor Rule. As part of that service, and again when I acted in the same role for the Uniform Trust Code Committee, I became enthralled by the elegance and perfection of the original Prudent Man Rule; a legal case ruling that had successfully guided the legal direction and scope of trust investments for 165 years. That ruling is central to the history of the Boston Trustee.

In 2012, my law school trusts and estates professor, John Langbein, the person who inspired me to enter the field, challenged me to prove why individual professional trustees were, and remain, prevalent in Boston and not in the rest of the country. My co-author, Heidi Seely, hired by Nichols & Pratt in 2010, joined me in finding the answer for my former professor – and so this project was born.

A search for hidden history in modern times is a fascinating journey. I have spent time wandering the stacks while learning the Boston Athenæum's arcane library filing systems, spent a glorious afternoon with my daughter Kate searching for mile markers on Route 138 in Canton, Milton and Mattapan, and have become very familiar with Google searches. I hope you enjoy what we have found.

THOMAS E. BATOR
Boston, Massachusetts

Introduction

The Boston Trustee is a distinct type. The term 'private trustee' only begins to outline him.[1]

IN HIS FIRST-RELEASED single *How 'Bout You*, country singer-songwriter Eric Church proudly proclaims that he doesn't have a "blue-blood trust fund" to support him.[2] Unfortunately for Mr. Church, this entire book is about blue-bloods and trust funds. In Boston, unlike anywhere else in the country, individual professional trustees practice trusteeship in a modern way under a tradition that extends back to the early 1800s. You might think of them as fine straw hat makers who still practice the art of millinery in small shops while 99% of all straw hats are now manufactured by multi-national companies by machine. While both hats may be excellent, they are nonetheless different.

This book tells the story of the Boston Trustees, individuals who act as trustees for families as their profession. It explores why they exist in Boston and not elsewhere in the country, and why they continue to be a relevant and excellent option for families and individuals who want their descendants to have both financial security and trusted advisors to support them through life.

In 1937, Donald Holbrook, a professional trustee from Boston, wrote a 38-page volume entitled *The Boston Trustee*. In his foreword, he wrote, "I am continually being asked by my friends outside of New England concerning the background of Boston Trusteeship, and have felt chagrined that my profession was not better known beyond my own locale. Hence this little volume."[3] In his book, Holbrook attempted to answer three questions: what was meant by the term "Boston Trustee," why did they only thrive in Boston, and how had individual professional trustees adapted to the changing times?

More than seventy-five years have passed since the publication of Holbrook's book, and the individual private professional trustee continues to exist and to thrive in Boston unlike anywhere else in this country. In 2012, by our informal count, an amount in excess of $30 billion was held in trust by Boston firms that we would characterize as Boston Trustee offices (including law firm trust departments). As Holbrook observed in 1937:

> Boston trustee practice has weathered many a
> gale by conducting itself in accordance with
> well tested principles. There is no indication
> that they will do more than adjust themselves
> to the tempo of the times as it may relate to
> proper management and not radically step
> outside of their traditional code and manner of
> performance.[4]

As we have researched the origins of the Boston Trustee, it has become clear that there is no one location where the original descriptions and source materials of the profession are collected and no one place where the essential principles of the Boston Trustee have been set forth. Many of the first Boston Trustees were practicing lawyers acting as trustees, a duality that continues in Boston as perhaps nowhere else in this country. The increasing concentration of trusteeship in a small number of national companies, several of which are publically traded, gives rise to the question of whether the individual professional trustee has a place in the fast-paced modern world.

This volume is our attempt to expand upon and update the work of Mr. Holbrook by: exploring the world of trusts and why the trustee is central to their success; giving a brief history of the Boston Trustee; defining it and tracing its essential characteristics; setting forth why we believe the Boston Trustee has thrived in Boston and not elsewhere; and arguing that the Boston Trustee – the individual professional trustee who views his or her role as that of a counselor in addition that of a fiduciary – continues to have a valid and valuable place in the world of trusts and trusteeship.

To help to unlock the opaque and often invisible world of trusts, we will use as examples the will and life of John McLean, both of which are famous, but also unknown. McLean's will gave rise to the most famous trust investment case in United States history and contained the bequest that gave rise to one of the best known psychiatric hospitals in the country. McLean's personal story gives context to our discussion of trusts and, we hope, will help unlock the subject by providing a real example of their use.

The Donor: John McLean

*In the name of
God, Amen.
I John McLean
of Boston in the
county of Suffolk
and Commonwealth
of Massachusetts,
Merchant, being
of sound and
disposing mind and
memory do make,
publish and declare,
this my last will
and testament,
in manner and
form following.*[1]

A TRUST IS AN ARRANGEMENT, usually in a written document, whereby a person, often referred to as the donor or settlor, transfers property to another person or institution, the trustee, to hold for the benefit of a third person or group of people, the beneficiaries. The trust itself can contain provisions, rules and powers, but it relies upon the law in statutes and cases for interpretation.

One could argue that the trust contained in the will of John McLean is the most important trust in United States history for the case law that arose from its interpretation. The case analyzing the investments made by the trustees of the McLean trust gave us the standard by which all trust investments are measured. McLean was the donor who set up the trust, wrote down the trust terms, and then died. The death of the donor is often an important factor for the type of trust we are discussing. After death, the donor is not able to tell us what he or she meant by the terms of the trust. He or she cannot help the trustee make decisions in difficult situations and cannot revise or amend the trust after his or her death. The donor leaves the trustee in his or her place.

John McLean's father, Hugh, was born in Ireland in 1724. Hugh McLean was a successful merchant in Maine partnering with James Boies to trade in England and the West Indies. Later he moved to Milton, Massachusetts, and became a partner with Boies in a paper manufacturing business and together they owned a paper mill in Mattapan, Massachusetts, that was later sold to McLean.[2] Papermaking was an essential business at this time and during the Revolutionary War there was a severe paper shortage. The commodity was so vital that when four apprentices who had paper-making expertise enlisted in the colonial army, Boies and McLean's petition to the Provisional Congress on May 15, 1775, to have them instead assigned to the paper mill was granted and on the same day, a prisoner in Worcester who was a paper maker was released to work in the Boies McLean mill.[3] Hugh McLean's business was so successful that when he died he had accumulated "a considerable fortune."[4]

Hugh McLean married Boies's daughter, Agnes, who gave birth to John in 1761. There is some debate as to where John was born and we do not even know the exact date of his birth. Josiah Quincy, in his history of Harvard College, states that McLean was born in "Georges, now Thomaston, Maine."[5]

Other sources with more specificity state that he was born in Milton, Massachusetts, where his mother's parents had settled.[6]

> [It] has been quite a disputed question whether Warren, Me., or Milton, Mass., is entitled to the honor of being the birthplace of John McLean, the benefactor of so many human sufferers; but this account of his mother's speedy departure, unless indeed he were born on board the vessel, seems to favor the claim of Milton. Still he might have been born in the unfurnished house.[7]

However, the Milton record of births does not list John McLean's birth in the Town.[8] We do know that John McLean was an only child and attended the Milton public schools.

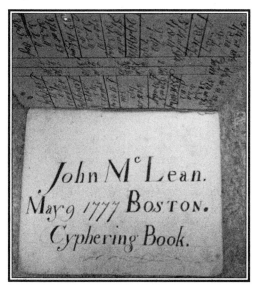

MILTON PUBLIC SCHOOL CYPHERING BOOK
OF JOHN MCLEAN, AGE 16

While John was not originally from the Boston elite, he, like many others in the fluidity of post-Revolutionary War Boston, was able to gain entry into Boston society with his "new" money. We do not know very much more about John until October 15, 1795, when he bought a house for $8,000 on the Charles Bulfinch designed Franklin Street Crescent.[9]

A fellow Bostonian described McLean at this time:

His handsome countenance and commanding
figure were very much admired, and the
magnetic quality of his social and genial
nature captivated those who had the honor
of his acquaintance or friendship. He was
rarely seen walking in the streets of Boston for
several years, having become afflicted with
the gout, which compelled him to ride in his
carriage whenever he desired an outing.[10]

On February 14, 1796, at King's Chapel, Boston, McLean married Ann Amory, one of the eleven children of John Amory. The Amorys were members of the Boston inner circle. McLean was a merchant. He partnered with Isaac Davenport and worked from offices on Long Wharf while establishing himself in Boston society, becoming a member of the Massachusetts (Boston) Chapter of the Masonic Society[11] and one of the original shareholders of the Manufacturers' and Mechanics' Bank in 1814 and the City Bank of Boston in 1822.[12]

It appears that McLean led a boom and bust merchant's life, his fortunes hitting a low at the end of the eighteenth century. "Business adversity embarrassed Mr. McLean during the latter part of the eighteenth century, which was caused by an unfortunate decree of the French council."[13] After the signing of Jay's Treaty in 1794 between the United States and England, the French government authorized the taking of American ships by French privateers. Between December of 1799 and January of 1800, eight ships whose insurance was in part underwritten by John McLean were taken by French privateers.[14] Some accounts state that McLean went bankrupt while others state that he almost went bankrupt, but was saved financially by the arrival of a ship thought lost. The United States Bankruptcy law was only in effect from June 2, 1800, through December 19, 1803, during McLean's lifetime, possibly explaining why he may not have gone through "official" bankruptcy. Eventually, he recovered and was able to pay off all of his creditors:

> A few years later he invited all of his creditors to a supper at the Exchange Coffee House, in Boston, where the sterling integrity which was the basis of his noble character manifested itself by a most pleasing and substantial act. When the guests assembled at the table every man found under his plate a check for the full amount of his debt, principal and interest.[15]

McLean continued his business ventures and it is said that he made $100,000 alone in a speculation on molasses at the time of the War of 1812.[16] John McLean died a wealthy and well-regarded man on October 23, 1823, leaving an estate of $228,120 (approximately $4.5 million in 2014 dollars).[17] His reputation at his death had matured to the point that it was said after his passing, "Mr. McLean was a truly noble specimen of a Boston Merchant."[18]

JOHN MCLEAN

When McLean died in 1823, he left a will dated August 13, 1821, as amended by a codicil dated September 18, 1822. The will was fourteen pages long, contained several cash gifts, two trusts for individuals, and two charitable trusts, and originally contained a massive drafting flaw that was fixed in the codicil. As far as we know its text is reproduced for the first time here on page 139.

McLean first gave his house and personal property, including his pew at the Federal Street Meeting House, to his "beloved wife Ann" outright. Next he gave Ann thirty-five thousand dollars (approximately $690,000 in 2014 dollars[19]) "to and for her own use and behoof forever." After these gifts, McLean established a trust for Ann and two charities and a separate trust for his nephew.

While simple in its terms, the trust for Ann and the charities spawned two Massachusetts Supreme Judicial Court cases, one of which shaped the entire Boston Trustee profession. These trusts can help us understand trusts and their uses in more general terms, as well as how the specific trusts of this time period helped to establish the particular Boston tradition of private professional trustees.

The Trust Document

'No, I'm not a czar,' the trustee said calmly,
'But I am given a certain amount of power.'[1]

T HE TRUSTEE MANAGES trust property as the legal owner of the property, but must do so for the benefit of the beneficiaries. Under traditional legal doctrine, the beneficiaries of the trust must be identifiable so that there is someone who may enforce the trust. More recently, trusts without identifiable beneficiaries have been allowed, such as trusts for pets, but these more modern statutes require that there be a person able to enforce the trust's provisions.[2] For charitable trusts, the charity, the state Attorney General, and in some states, the donor, are able to enforce the trust.

Trusts can be of long or short duration. Some trusts are established to last merely until the beneficiary reaches twenty-one years of age, but other trusts are meant to last for over one hundred years. Trusts can be very specific or general as to their terms, and can be established for many different purposes. These purposes tend to revolve around protecting beneficiaries or property (and sometimes property *from* beneficiaries). Today, tax planning to defer or minimize various taxes is the impetus behind many trusts. Some trusts allow the trustee to distribute funds for any purpose in the trustee's sole discretion while others dictate payment terms down to the exact amount, date, and purpose. Often the trust income must be paid out, but usually the principal may only be paid out in the trustee's discretion.

In the trust McLean established for his wife, Ann, John McLean is the *donor*. Ann Amory McLean's brother and cousin, Jonathan and Francis Amory, are named as *trustees*, and Ann, Harvard College, and the Massachusetts General Hospital are the *beneficiaries*. Fifty thousand dollars, or, as we will see, fifty thousand *invested* dollars is the *trust property*. The last important elements for a trust are the *trust document* and *the law* that governs the trust.

Usually the trust is contained in a written document, but oral trusts have been upheld as legal in some cases, including a trust that held shares in the Boston Braves baseball team.[3] Unfortunately, written trusts are often long, complex legal documents. Some of this is due to the drafting lawyer's legitimate attempt to precisely set forth what is to happen, keeping in mind that the trust provisions must take into account that the trust may last for over one hundred years. Too often, however, poor drafting, legalese and an inability to edit make trusts incomprehensible to the lay reader and sometimes even to other lawyers. Often trusts do not obey the normal conventions of clear writing that would put topics together that should be congruent. Words are often used at the front of the document and then defined at the back. For example, there are trusts that contain the requirement to pay the income to a beneficiary on page one of the document that thirty pages later provide that wherever a trustee must pay income to a beneficiary, the trustee also has the power to pay principal. Why not say that on page one?

The trustees in McLean's trust were required to pay Ann the trust's "profits and income" in quarterly or semi-annual payments. Upon Ann's death, one-half of the property was to pass to Harvard College and one-half to the Massachusetts General Hospital. During the early nineteenth century, when Bostonians were trying to raise funds for a hospital, "Mr. John Lowell and Mr. John McLean had married sisters, and the latter having no children and a large estate needed little persuasion to devise a large part of his means for the purpose."[4] Considering the fact that McLean did not attend Harvard, it is interesting that he left such a large portion of his estate to the college. We do not know why he made the gift. The trust's detail is devoted to describing a Professorship of Ancient and Modern History at Harvard that still exists to this day.

The McLean trust contained a typical "split" of beneficial interests, with Ann to receive income for her life and the charities the remainder on her death. This type of trust can be challenging to administer because the trustees' duty of loyalty is to all beneficiaries, and the balancing of interests is often difficult. For this trust, with non-professional family trustees, it is not surprising that the charities would come to feel that the trustees had favored family to the detriment of the charities.

In his trust for his namesake nephew, John McLean Bethune, McLean gave the trustees discretion to invest and distribute the trust fund to John. Bethune was the older son of Ann McLean's sister, Mary. Whether or not due to the fund, Bethune ended up well-educated, attending the Boston Latin School, Harvard College, and Harvard Law School before becoming a successful lawyer.

After a gift to the Boston Female Asylum of $500, the final disposition by McLean was the creation of two separate $2,000 funds, one to the minister and deacons of the Congregational Society in Milton and one to the minister and deacons of the Congregational Society on Federal Street, Boston, in each case to be held in trust with the interest and income of the fund to be paid in the winter months to people of the parish who were "not paupers." We do not know why this limitation was added. McLean specifically set forth the process and timing of the vote as to who should receive the funds (November), required that the amounts and recipients be recorded in a book kept for that purpose, and even specified the manner of breaking tie votes. This is an example of how trusts can be as flexible as their donors' and drafters' imaginations.

The trustee has a great deal to do with the success of the trust and the experience of its beneficiaries. Given a reasonably drafted document, if there is any discretion left to the trustee, it is the decisions made by the trustee that matter to the experience of the beneficiaries more than the inert document. Long-lasting trusts can have many trustees during their existence, each with his or her idiosyncrasies, strengths, and weaknesses.

The power vested in trustees and their importance to beneficiaries makes an understanding of the Boston Trustee critical to determining its place among the choices of individual and corporate trustees available to donors today.

The Boston Trustee

*Trusteeship in Boston is more than a profession
and the true Boston Trustee is more than a
professional man. He is an institution.*[1]

THE TRUSTEES of the trust for Ann McLean
and Jonathan and Francis Amory were merchants like John McLean, not professional
trustees. At the time of the signing of John's will in
1821, there were few, if any, professional individual
trustees in Boston and certainly there were no corporate trustees. Then, as now, there were many individuals who acted as trustees for their families or
for friends. Early trustees in England and America
were most often just unpaid trustworthy individuals.
Chantal Stebbins described the role as follows:

> Any man – relatively rarely, it will be seen, woman
> – who took on trusteeship for a member of his
> family was thus playing – and was seen to be
> playing – his part in the preservation not only of

the family interests but of the wider social order.... Trusteeship was an act of true affection and esteem, a demonstrable adherence to the social and moral codes, and as such is ensured the respect of the trustee's own social class.[2]

Unfortunately, very few families needing a trustee have a ready-made family member sufficiently trained and interested in taking the job. Trusteeship, whether one is paid or not, is hard work. One current Boston Trustee describes his profession as one-third investing, one-third legal work, and one-third psychiatry. For this volume, we are only interested in individual *professional* trustees; people who specialize in trusteeship as a profession. They are paid for the services they provide, hold themselves out as specialists in that business, and undertake the profession as their primary work.

The Boston Trustee was born from a confluence of economic, historical, and societal elements specific to Boston in the early to mid-1800s. "He is a particular kind of private trustee, the product of that unique social and economic environment which gave shape and character to nineteenth-century Boston."[3] A Boston Trustee not only holds himself out to the outside world as a *professional* trustee, but also believes that his or her duties extend beyond merely the investment of the trust assets. Serving as counselor to the trust's beneficiaries while carrying out the wishes (both express and implied) of the donor is the "extra" that distinguishes the Boston Trustee from the typical trustee. "A Boston Trustee, he is far more than the executor of estates. He has served heirs in the role of father, counseling, advising and watchdogging the family inheritance."[4]

The prototypical Boston Trustee is seen by his peers and clients as something akin to a trusted friend — someone who understands the donor and beneficiaries and who can be trusted to care not only for their finances, but all aspects of their lives. There are hundreds of stories of the personal services performed by Boston Trustees; many of them are highly entertaining, but that would be a different book for another time. For now, it may be sufficient to say that Boston Trustees have been asked to meet potential spouses of young rich beneficiaries and opine on the suitability of the match, to transfer cash to remote parts of Europe when beneficiaries are robbed, to refill furnaces with coal in the middle of the night, and to mediate between angry family members. In one family, the sister calls her brother "Richard" when she agrees with him, but is heard to use the shorter version of his name when she disagrees. The trustee, with a position in the midst of the family, can be put into difficult situations.

As E. Sohier Welch, a prominent Boston Trustee, said:

One reason why we shall never go out of business ... is that the size of the estate we handle makes very little difference in the amount of service we give to it .... People come to us for advice on the most intimate and confidential matters .... Now and again we have to talk like Dutch uncles — never a pleasure but none the less a necessity. Under these circumstances the older families naturally wish to deal with someone whom they know, someone who moves in the same social environment and has a similarity of tastes and traditions.[5]

In the beginning, almost all Boston Trustees were individuals of established Boston ancestry, serving clientele of similar ancestry and traditions. One prominent trustee noted that, "Old Boston families have a strong inclination to deal with people bound to them by social ties."[6] Today, while many Boston Trustees do not hail from old-line Boston families, they carry on the traditions of duty, propriety, quiet dignity, and service that were the hallmarks of the profession's founders.

The first professional trustees in America were lawyers. Well-thought-of in the community, they knew about trusts through their work and were generally honorable. As such, the Boston Trustee has been compared to the English solicitor because of parallel elements in the two occupations; however, there are notable differences between them. While both professions serve as counselors and advisors to their clients, the Boston Trustee is often, but not always, a lawyer. Solicitors and Boston Trustees both manage the funds of their clients; however, in 1830 the Boston Trustee was granted the authority by the courts to invest as a "prudent man" would, while at that time the English solicitor was more restricted in his investment powers.[7]

While this particular combination of attorney, investor, and advisor may be practiced to a modest extent in other areas of the country, it has clearly flourished in Boston where it continues today in the same tradition of those original Bostonians who set the standard of what it means to be a Boston Trustee. In our view, the rise and continuation of the individual professional trustee in Boston and not elsewhere was a product of: (1) the history of the city, including Boston's early strength as a financial center and the unique close family, commercial, and social ties of Boston merchant society, (2) a favorable legal backdrop, (3) a lenient and opportunity-rich trust investing environment, and (4) the good fortune of individual trustees to have been successful and established before corporate trustees had become fully entrenched as competitors. "Eventually, the trustee became so venerated that, when the head of the family was about to expire, the proper Bostonian would say: 'One must first call the doctor, then the mortician and then the trustee.'"[8]

Origins of the Boston Trustee

Mr. Dexter's father used to observe that he never invested in anything he could not see from his office window.[1]

T HERE ARE NO contemporaneous identifications of the earliest "Boston Trustee." There are no recorded sightings of the first trustee who claimed to be a "professional" trustee, let alone claimed to be a "Boston Trustee." We are left to infer that the rise of the Boston Trustee was one of evolution and the result of a multitude of factors. Donald Holbrook decided to write *The Boston Trustee* in 1937 partly due to the absence of an historical record. Unfortunately, he failed to be precise about the profession's origins:

> History and biography show that men of
> substance turned most readily to their doctor
> or lawyer on confidential matters. Certainly
> this was true before the age of specialization,
> when friendly and personal association

frequently laid the basis for complete
confidence. It was natural, therefore, for
the man of property to turn to his lawyer
not only to draw up the vehicle which
should provide the transmission of his wealth
to future generations, but also to assume a
position of guidance and responsibility
relative to it.[2]

The history of the Boston Trustee is exceptionally difficult to unearth because it is, by definition, the history of a business that was meant to be private. The families for whom the individual trustee worked valued that privacy. Confidentiality was considered and still remains an essential characteristic and key responsibility of a trustee.

It is a well ingrained part of private trustee culture that private trustees do not, by and large, advertise: "Boston trustees arc a secretive lot. They not only don't advertise but they are most reluctant to tell you anything about their business."[3] Boston Trustee Philip Dexter, writing to his Harvard classmates for his fiftieth reunion, downplayed his profession:

Some people have been good enough to want
me to take care of their property, which has
been during the past fifteen years sufficiently
absorbing to preclude other occupations.
Except for a couple of short trips to Europe, I
have been sticking to that job, and although it
interests me, I don't know how to tell about it
in a way that will interest any one else. There
is not much romantic excitement in other
people's coupons.[4]

Even in 1992, when shown an advertisement for another trustee office in the Boston Symphony program, one Boston Trustee was seen raising his eyebrow and shaking his head. This secrecy was in part due to legal ethical rules that forbade lawyers from advertising. Most of the early Boston Trustees were lawyers. Advertising lawyers risked disbarment until 1977 when the United States Supreme Court upheld lawyer advertising as protected free speech under the First Amendment of the Constitution.[5]

It is also likely that the personal nature of the selection of a Boston Trustee made general advertisements disadvantageous. A general solicitation in a newspaper or magazine would be more likely to draw unsuitable clients than desirable ones. As one Boston Trustee put it, "We are occasionally obliged to turn away large and profitable estates because they are not in our line."[6]

While tracing the first Boston Trustees and their firms is difficult, it is clear their presence was felt in Boston from the early to mid 1800s. A 1935 article in the *Boston Evening Transcript* identified the earliest of the Boston Trustees as "William Minot, George Morey, Charles P. Curtis, Charles G. Loring, and Edward D. Sohier."[7] Although these men all lived and worked in Boston in the first half of the nineteenth century, we find conflicting evidence as to their roles as Boston Trustees.

We can find little detailed information about George Morey's trusteeship practice. He is listed twice as "trustee" of property in the 1848 tax rolls of the City of Boston.[8] Additionally, in describing Morey and William Minot, a popular 1846 pamphlet listing the wealthy members of Boston society with brief biographies, noted that "Both the foregoing have acquired fortunes by diligent attention to their profession, and fidelity to those who have entrusted business in their hands."[9]

Charles P. Curtis lived from 1792 until 1864 and his practice is also alluded to in the 1846 pamphlet: "Lawyer; son of a Boston merchant of the late firm of Curtis & Loring. His extensive family connection early introduced him into a lucrative and respectable business."[10] In Curtis's obituary, the personal nature of his trusteeship was noted: "He entered into the business of his clients, and espoused their interests, with hearty zeal, so that his friends were his clients and his clients were his friends."[11] A long line of professional trustees descends from Charles P. Curtis. A 1959 article about Boston Trustees was written by Charles P. Curtis, a descendant of the original Charles, and a more recent Curtis descendant was a trusts and estates lawyer with an extensive trust practice at Choate, Hall & Stewart.[12]

While Charles G. Loring, another of those named as an early Boston Trustee, was a very famous lawyer and judge, we do not see other references to his profession as trustee. Loring's inventory and accounts for the Boott family are in the public record, but we do not know if he was acting as a family friend or as a professional in that matter.[13] We find references to Charles's son, Caleb William Loring, acting as a professional trustee. Caleb graduated from Harvard College in 1839. "In early life he had a large general practice and tried many important insurance cases, and afterward he became a trustee and attorney for estates, wills and trusts, representing a large amount of property."[14]

In 1823, the year of McLean's death, *The Boston Directory*, a publication that listed all Boston residents and their professions, did not list a single person with the profession of "trustee."[15] Instead, the men referred to elsewhere as leading trustees of the time are listed almost uniformly as "counsellor." Even as late as 1873, no person is listed in *The Directory* with the occupation of "trustee," and leading trustees are still listed as "counsellor," reinforcing both the difficulty of tracing the profession and the conclusion that these men did not choose to advertise or reveal their profession to non-clients.[16]

While trustees did not describe themselves as trustees in public, in the tax rolls we can see a more accurate listing of trusteeship and the profession. The 1848 City of Boston Tax rolls show 112 individuals identified as trustees with total real estate holdings of $1,736,500 and personal property totaling $2,023,300. As one would expect, where taxes are concerned, the reporting of trusteeship is more transparent, and we can see people identified elsewhere as professional trustees all listed with trust property: Nathaniel and Jonathan Ingersoll Bowditch, Charles P. Curtis, Charles G. Loring, William Minot, and George Morey.[17]

Interestingly, the son of the first mayor of Boston, Josiah Quincy, Jr., who was also a mayor of Boston, is listed as trustee six times in the 1848 tax rolls, more than any other person. In 1846, he was described as "Son of the foregoing; now mayor of Boston. He married a lady of property, and has held many lucrative trusts and guardianships, by which he has accumulated a large fortune. Of unimpeachable integrity, affable manners and fluent speech, he has been much in public life."[18]

It is also possible to trace the history of early Boston Trustees by looking at the lineage of present-day trustee offices. The current trustee office of Rice, Heard & Bigelow, Inc., traces its roots to George Richards Minot and the Minot family of trustees. "When George Richards Minot opened his Court Street office in 1782 the business of trustees was the care of testamentary trusts, property left to them by will for the benefit of persons named in the will, generally the wife and children of the testator."[19]

Although George Richards Minot was a very prominent member of the Boston legal community, we have found no other specific references to his profession as a trustee. Minot was a judge of probate for Suffolk County from 1792 until his death in 1802. He was also chief justice of the Suffolk Court of Common Pleas and a judge of the municipal court in the town of Boston. He was clerk of the House of Representatives from 1782 until 1791.

However, his son, William, born in 1783, clearly was a professional trustee:

> For many years he was one of Boston's most distinguished lawyers, especially in that department relating to trusts, wills, and estates, and his services were constantly in demand as executor or trustee where large interests were involved. Those sterling traits of integrity, method, industry, and fidelity, inherited from his father, particularly fitted him for such duties, and he acquired a reputation second to no man in this connection.[20]

William Minot was described by his contemporary, Charles A. Welch, as someone who "had a very extensive & profitable charge of Trust estates & was an excellent man."[21] Minot was also the treasurer of the Benjamin Franklin trust fund for Boston from 1811 until 1866. (The Franklin Funds are discussed later in a separate chapter.)

William Minot's son, William, Jr., was born in 1817 and was admitted to the Suffolk bar in 1841. William, Jr. seems to have almost exclusively acted as a trustee and executor:

> He was in active legal business for more than fifty years, and had the confidence of so many people, that, though he had no conspicuously large trusts, he at one time held more property in his own office and in his single control than any financial institution in Boston, and equal in amount to a hundredth part of the assessed value of all the property in the city.[22]

The Minot family continued to participate in the profession of trusteeship for generations.

The modern day Loring, Wolcott & Coolidge Office traces its roots back to Nathaniel Bowditch.[23] Augustus P. Loring, Jr., a private trustee himself, claimed that Nathaniel Bowditch was the first true *professional* trustee because, according to Loring, "he probably was the person who conceived the idea that each Trust should be kept rigidly *independent* of the trustee's personal funds."[24]

While Bowditch's activities as a trustee and as the Actuary of the Massachusetts Hospital Life Insurance Company are of greatest interest to us, he is renowned worldwide in the context of navigation and mathematics. Bowditch was born March 26, 1773, in Salem, Massachusetts. He came from very modest circumstances, but went to school at age seven and became recognized for his great mind, particularly in math. At age ten he went to work for a cooper until he was twelve when he was apprenticed to a ship-chandlery shop.

On January 11, 1795, he went on his first ocean voyage. In the late eighteenth century, accurate time was not available on ships. Bowditch recognized the need for a simple method to determine lunar distances and derived a new method for doing so during this first voyage. John Hamilton Moore's *The Practical Navigator* was the leading text on navigation when Bowditch went to sea, but Bowditch determined early in the trip that Moore's text contained important errors and commenced the recomputation of several important tables. On hearing of his findings, the book's publisher hired Bowditch and others to check Moore's work. Bowditch proceeded to edit two editions of *The New American Practical Navigator.* By the third edition, he had corrected it so completely and found so many errors that it was published under his name and it is this work for which he is known worldwide as "Nat the Navigator."[25]

Bowditch's son, referring to *The New American Practical Navigator* in his memoir of his father, asserted that "[f]rom that time to the present, it has been exclusively used by every ship-master who has sailed from this country, and its tables and rules have been adopted in the works used in England and elsewhere."[26] The United States Navy thought the work so important that they purchased the copyright and have maintained the work ever since.

Bowditch went on five voyages, the last as supercargo and part owner on the *Putnam* (coincidentally, the last name of the judge whose legal decision became the basis for judging all trust investing, the so-called "Prudent Man Rule"). The supercargo managed cargo for its owners while on the ship, sold the merchandise when it arrived at the destination port, and bought and received goods to be carried on the return voyage. Supercargoes "managed their finances by maintaining *separate* entities, so that a loss or gain on *one* portion of the cargo would not affect *another*."[27]

Loring believed that Bowditch's seafaring experience as a supercargo for Salem merchant ships and his natural mathematical and accounting instincts informed his later profession as Actuary and trustee. Along with two others, Bowditch was a trustee of the Orne Fund which was established in 1817 by Eliza Wetmore for the support of the Ministers of the First Church in Salem. Loring notes that:

> Up until the time the Orne Fund was set up, men who held money in trust merely added it to their own funds, but maintained separate records. Bowditch felt this was not the proper way to handle trusts because if they went bankrupt, then all the funds shared in the financial disaster and were lost to those entitled to them."[28]

While an acknowledged genius and the father of American navigation, Bowditch was not a typical example of the early Boston Trustee; he was not from the inner circle of Boston families, nor did he attend Harvard College.[29] While of course not every early Boston Trustee attended Harvard, most of them did, as was expected by Boston Brahmin society. "By the 1830s, Harvard had become a central mecha-

nism for socializing the sons of elite families—as
well as for recruiting talented and ambitious young
men into commercial and eleemosynary enterprises
in which they were interested."[30]

NATHANIEL BOWDITCH

Bowditch, intelligent, famously honest, and always
correct in his dealings, also believed in the personal
service aspect of trusteeship. This became the hall-
mark of a Boston Trustee. Bowditch was particularly solicitous of those without the experience to
manage their own finances. Bowditch is said to have

required women who had annuities with the Massachusetts Hospital Life Insurance Company when he was its Actuary to come in person to his offices to receive their payments so that "he might himself give them any explanations and information that they desired."[31]

Bowditch's second son, Jonathan Ingersoll Bowditch, followed in his father's path and began his business life as a supercargo for Ropes & Ward, noted East India merchants. Jonathan was named the President of the American Insurance Company in Boston and served in that role until 1864. He, too, was a professional trustee:

> Mr. Bowditch for many years had the management of large and important private trusts, especially of estates of widows and orphans, – a charge in which equal reliance was placed, and never misplaced, in his painstaking fidelity, his far-seeing prudence, and his financial skill.[32]

The private trustee office of Welch & Forbes, LLC, views the founding of a law partnership between Charles Alfred Welch and Edward Dexter Sohier in 1838 as the firm's beginning. Both men were lawyers. Welch was a member of one of Boston's oldest families, and, although he is not mentioned as a trustee in histories of the Suffolk County bar, his son, Francis Clarke Welch, who joined the firm in 1871, was said to have been Boston's largest taxpayer (presumably due to his large real estate holdings as trustee) and one of Boston's leading professional trustees.[33] While we can find no references to Sohier's trust "business," an obituary mentions his "exceedingly sagacious investments."[34] A well-known attorney, he was one of the lawyers for Professor John White Webster in his famous 1850 trial for the murder of Boston Brahmin Dr. George Parkman whose dismembered and partially burned body was found at the Harvard Medical School by a janitor after he had inexplicably been missing for a week. Parkman had lent Webster money and, when Webster sold property he had mortgaged to secure his loan, Parkman sought to force repayment. Webster was convicted and was later hanged on August 30, 1850.

Another early Boston Trustee, William Sohier Dexter, began his practice in 1848. "His great ability as an investor gave him a high place among the trustees of Boston, and as director of many large financial enterprises."[35] Dexter was the father of the famous Boston Trustee, Philip Dexter, whose death in 1934 prompted an article about Boston Trustees.[36] According to Charles P. Curtis, a Boston Trustee himself, Dexter also trained Robert H. Gardiner as a trustee.[37] In 1928, Gardiner, who had opened his original trust office in the 1880s, came to the conclusion that he needed to incorporate the office to serve the trusts and beneficiaries under his care in perpetuity and with adequate investment support. "[H]e became assured that the need for the personal type of trustee is not only as pressing as ever but is growing rapidly."[38] This firm was Fiduciary Trust Company, which continues today.

One of the themes one can see with almost all of these early examples is that trusteeship quickly became a family business, with fathers passing on trusteeships to their sons. Although it is lengthy, the 1950 description by Augustus P. Loring, Jr. of the one hundred and fourteen year history of his trusteeship practice is indicative of the profession and worth citing in full. After discussing Nathaniel Bowditch, Loring continued:

His son, Jonathan Ingersoll Bowditch, started business about 1836 and, according to the records, acted as Trustee along with his duties as President of the American Insurance Company, a position he held from 1826 to 1864. Jonathan retired from business in 1881, and died in 1889. His son, Charles P. Bowditch, was associated more or less with him from 1864, and took over the trust business his father had, to which he added enormously, and acted as Trustee, more or less, until his death, on June 1, 1921. His brother, Alfred Bowditch, my father-in-law, likewise was associated with him; and they afterwards maintained a common office although they had their separate office forces, without connection in a business way except as co-trustees. Alfred Bowditch had a large trust business, and he died on February 22, 1918. I, myself, came into the office of Alfred Bowditch as a clerk in the autumn of 1912 and filled various positions, from office boy to bookkeeper, until the death of Alfred Bowditch; at which time I took over a part of Mr. Bowditch's trust business, approximately two-thirds of which went out of the office at the time to other co-trustees, as I was considered inexperienced and was rather a young man. I shared an office with Charles P. Bowditch and later with his son, Ingersoll Bowditch, who took over the whole of his father's business on June 1,

1921, although he had a considerable business of his own. We shared offices until April 1927, when Ingersoll Bowditch decided to part company because he needed more space and wished to maintain an office of his own. It was then that I set up an office of my own and moved it to the offices of Loring, Coolidge, Noble & Boyd, at 40 State Street in Boston. As my father's office combined with Gaston, Snow, Saltonstall, Hunt & Rice, we formed a Trust Department which I now head. Meanwhile, Ingersoll Bowditch died, and I took over a considerable amount of his business; so you might say I am the continuation of the Bowditch office.[39]

In many cases, a trust instrument provides that the trustee can name his or her successor, sometimes with the consent of the beneficiaries. In other cases, familiarity with and trust in a father would prompt an empowered beneficiary to name the trustee's son a successor. This would particularly be true if the son was "known" due to schooling and bloodline:

Fathers planned a trustee career for their sons with a thoroughness which they considered essential where financial matters are involved. Adequate experience and essential training were provided before the responsibility of trusteeship was dropped on younger shoulders. Many outstanding names in Boston trustee practice are witnesses to the tradition handed from father to son, which assured thorough and competent handling of capital entrusted to their charge.[40]

The story of how Donald Holbrook himself became a Boston Trustee is instructive, though not traditional, for he did not follow a father into the business. Holbrook did attend a New England prep school and Harvard College, but did not complete his Harvard education due to his service in World War I. Holbrook began his professional career in 1919 as a bond salesman with Coffin and Burr where he was very successful earning commissions for the firm through the sale of bonds. He learned the bond business, however, with an objective in mind. "I had studied the history and traditions of the Boston private trustee and my ultimate goal was to become a member of this profession; hopefully with a little more modern outlook, yet without breaking the tradition."[41] Holbrook was one of the first officers of Franklin Management Corporation which was established to provide investment advisory services to clients of Coffin and Burr. When Coffin and Burr began to doubt its backing of Franklin Management Corporation, Holbrook started his own business as a private trustee and investor and "in the passage of a few years my trust practice grew substantially with its increasing financial rewards."[42]

In reviewing the beginnings of the various offices that evolved into current Boston Trustee firms, we see that the origins of the business is murky at best. We can only assume that it was initially the reputations of the men involved earned from their expertise, financial acumen, and competence that led with increasing frequency to their nomination as trustees by tight-knit Boston Brahmin society. As these men gained more business, and relationships became accepted and formalized, they then handed that business off to their sons, and so a new profession was born.

The Property:
Economic and Social Backdrop

*As the first city to make large amounts of money,
Boston was also the first city to grow preoccupied
with conserving it.*[1]

W HEN JOHN MCLEAN DIED, almost one-
half of his estate consisted of shares in
the Boston Manufacturing Company
and the Merrimack Manufacturing Company. The
executors of the estate funded the $50,000 trust for
Mrs. McLean with nine shares of each company,
which they listed in their account as worth more
than half of the initial $50,000 trust fund. Shares
of each company were valued on the executors' inventory at their $1,000 per share par value plus, as
the executors put it, "say" a 40% appreciation, for a

total value of $25,200.

If there is a theme that describes Boston society of the early 1800s, it is an intense formal and informal control exerted on and by its members. This need for control is somewhat ironic given the speculative nature of the businesses that allowed for the economic rise of Boston, but it is present in all of the interactions among members of Boston society at that time. The men who lived in Boston and organized its economic engines of wealth, sometimes referred to as the Boston Associates,[2] lived together, connected their families through marriage, and tended to use the corporate form to control their businesses. By 1830 it was clear that trusts could hold corporate stock with limited liability for the trust and its beneficiaries. The control that was gained by the use of company stock owned by long-term trusts and managed by trusted members of Brahmin society proved irresistible to the Boston Associates.

We will continue to use the term "Boston Associates" to identify the group that developed the textile business around Boston and ascended into the upper class. The more common and general term used today for a member of the Boston upper class is "Boston Brahmin," a term Dr. Oliver Wendell Holmes, himself a member of the Boston elite,[3] is credited with coining in 1859 in his serialized story in *The Atlantic Monthly* magazine that became his novel *Elsie Venner: A Romance of Destiny:*

> What we mean by 'aristocracy' is merely the richer part of the community.... Some of these great folks are really well-bred, some of them are only purse-proud and assuming, — but they

form a class, and are named as above in the
common speech....

There is, however in New England, an
aristocracy, if you chose to call it so, which has
a far greater character of permanence. It has
grown to be a caste, — not in any odious sense,
— but, by the repetition of the same influences
generation after generation, it has acquired a
distinct organization and physiognomy....
He comes of the *Brahmin caste of New
England*. This is the harmless, inoffensive,
untitled aristocracy referred to, and which
many readers will at once acknowledge.[4]

Two economic factors in the early 1800s made trusts
and trusteeship by reliable trustees a necessity for
Boston society. First, with the end of the War of 1812,
Boston enjoyed a tremendous economic growth spurt
that created a society of prosperous merchants who
wanted to ensure that their families were cared for
and their wealth would not be squandered. Second,
the sources of their wealth, namely the manufacturing companies that were generating and expanding
that wealth, needed protection and good management upon the death of the original owner. Trusts
and trustees could provide that care and protection.

Boston was founded in 1630 by Governor John
Winthrop after a failed attempt to settle in what we
now call Charlestown due to its lack of fresh water.
Boston became a city in 1822 and its first mayor was
Josiah Quincy.

BOSTON BICENTENNIAL
TIME CAPSULE CONTAINER
*"To Mayor of Boston
To be opened on September 17, 1930"*

Boston's wealth and early prominence were built on its port, which ensured its maritime success. "Unlike New York, Philadelphia or even Baltimore, Boston appears to have been overwhelmingly oriented to trade and fishing. As late as 1840, the census reports of Boston had 10,813 people in the ocean-going professions and only 5,333 people in manufacturing."[5] This is in stark contrast to New York City and other Massachusetts cities like Lowell and Waltham, where manufacturing dominated.

However, after early and explosive growth, the port of Boston declined. "In 1821, 21 percent of American's imports and exports were handled by Boston and 29 percent by New York. Twenty years later, New York's share was up to 43 percent and Boston's was down to 10 percent."[6] In the face of this decline, one would have expected the city to have declined, but, in fact, the opposite occurred. In 1800, Boston's population was 25,000, a number, when looked at from a modern Bostonian's perspective, is just a bit larger than the capacity of the TD Garden where the Celtics and Bruins play, and smaller than the capacity of Fenway Park. By 1846, that population had grown to 120,000, about twice the size of a full Gillette Stadium, home of the New England Patriots. By 1870, 250,000 people lived in Boston. The decade with the greatest population growth in Boston between 1790 and 1900 was the 1830s, when the population grew by 51%. It was not just that there were more people in Boston – they were richer too. In 1840, only a handful of individuals were worth more than $1 million. By 1890, that number was 400.[7]

While Boston's presence as a port was declining, its control over shipping was in fact increasing. Between 1811 and 1851, the share of registered tonnage owned by New Englanders increased from 45 percent to 58 percent.[8] "Yankee ships spread their sails in the harbors of the world. Coins of nearly every nation under heaven found their way into Boston counting houses."[9]

After Boston maritime interests, textiles provided a second stage to New England economic growth. In 1813, the Boston Manufacturing Company built a cotton mill nine miles west of Boston in Waltham, which began a transformation of the Massachusetts economy. Prior to that time, English cloth was both of higher quality and cheaper than American cloth. In "a stunning act of industrial piracy,"[10] Francis Cabot Lowell, a wealthy Boston merchant, travelled to England in 1810, took tours of English mills, and memorized every piece of machinery he saw.[11] At the time of Lowell's trip to England, British law both prohibited the emigration of skilled textile workers and imposed heavy fines for exporting models or drawings of textile machinery. Lowell's bags were searched twice for designs and plans when he left England.[12] When he returned, the War of 1812 commenced, shutting off the flow of English cloth to America. Lowell decided to build an American factory using as models the more developed English machinery whose designs he had memorized.

Using Lowell's descriptions of what he had seen in England, Paul Moody, a mechanic, created the Waltham Power Loom, allowing the Boston Manufacturing Company to produce cloth of higher quality than that made in England at only a slight price disadvantage. Despite a depression in 1817, the Boston Manufacturing Company's business continued to grow unabated as its capital was large enough to allow it to survive economic dips. Dividends to shareholders from the Boston Manufacturing Company averaged 19.25% from 1817 to 1820 and increased to 27.5% in 1822.[13]

BOSTON MANUFACTURING COMPANY

The Property: Economic and Social Backdrop

After building three mills in Waltham, the men who organized the Boston Manufacturing Company, realizing that they needed a larger platform to produce textiles, formed the Merrimack Manufacturing Company and moved production twenty miles northeast to Lowell, Massachusetts. Other Boston Associates quickly followed suit and Lowell became a booming mill town. The largest mills, whose control was owned by a small handful of interrelated extended families, "produced an embarrassment of riches, a flood of wealth that grew faster than it could be spent. Funds were poured into new ventures: railroads, banks, real estate, iron, shipping and lumber. But these only yielded more profits."[14] During the 51 years after 1835, the so-called "Baker sample" textile companies in Waltham and Lowell averaged an 8.4 percent return on net worth.[15]

BOSTON ASSOCIATE TEXTILE COMPANY DIVIDENDS AND PROFITS

Year	Profits (% of Standard Net Worth)	Dividends (as % of Paid-in Capital Stock)
1836	14.80%	11.17%
1837	7.60%	11.35%
1838	3.70%	0.00%
1839	14.10%	8.03%
1840	4.20%	7.45%
1841	7.90%	7.36%
1842	3.20%	8.50%
1843	2.30%	2.89%
1844	19.10%	12.20%
1845	17.10%	16.99%
1846	18.20%	22.32%

MCGOULDRICK DATA ON NEW ENGLAND TEXTILE COMPANIES.[16]

With the creation of a new industry, the Boston Associates also needed a source of steady capital for their companies. The Massachusetts Hospital Life Insurance Company, known as "the savings bank for the wealthy,"[17] played a key role both in financing and in retaining tight control over the textile industry. The Massachusetts Hospital Life Insurance Company (the "Company") was initially founded in 1818 to help the finance the Massachusetts General Hospital. The Company was chartered on February 24, 1818. Under the terms of the charter, the Company was required to pay the Hospital one-third of the net profits of its life insurance business so long as it held a monopoly on the sale of life insurance or until another company was chartered that did not have to share its profits.[18]

In August of 1823, the Company's organizers hired Nathaniel Bowditch to become its first "Actuary" (the equivalent of its Chief Executive Officer). Bowditch had experience with life insurance as President of the Essex Fire & Marine Insurance Company of Salem. Simultaneously, at Bowditch's suggestion, the Legislature revised the Company's charter to broaden its powers of investment and to permit it to receive "property in trust for minors and others on such terms and conditions as may be mutually agreed upon by the Corporation and the person creating such trusts."[19]

The Company's Proposals promised to invest "always in view of the safety of Capital, rather than the greatness of the income."[20] Thus, under its original investment policy, the Company limited its investments to the debt of the United States and the Commonwealth of Massachusetts, stock in a federal bank or a bank incorporated in Massachusetts, and the purchase of rents and mortgages on real estate.[21] Accordingly, the Company could not invest directly in textile stocks. However, the Company's Committee of Finance (which was almost entirely made up of members of the Boston Associates) was able to stretch those rules by making loans to the Boston Manufacturing Company and other textile companies where the collateral was low or where the companies' directors personally put up the required collateral. Often textile loans were made on an on-demand basis, rather than with a term, an arrangement that certainly was more flexible for the borrower.[22] Nathan Appleton, perhaps the most preeminent of the Boston Associates, borrowed from the Massachusetts Hospital Life Insurance Company no fewer than thirty times before 1840[23]:

Beginning with its first significant loan of $20,000 to the Boston Manufacturing Co. in 1826 . . . the MHLIC became the largest supplier of loans to the New England textile industry and remained so throughout the nineteenth century. Every one of the textile mills or related companies with outstanding loans from the MHLIC in 1855 had a director linking both boards, suggesting that personal connections were channels of economic influence.[24]

In 1839, the Massachusetts Hospital Life Insurance Company was granted an amendment to its charter regularizing some of its practices and loosening collateral restrictions.[25] Beginning in 1845, textile loans increased dramatically: "According to the Massachusetts census of 1855, the MHLIC was supplying half of the capital invested in the cotton textile industry and an even greater percentage of the capital in the woolen textile industry."[26]

Over the next decade, the Massachusetts Hospital Life Insurance Company made 407 loans of which 168 went to the textile industry.[27] While these investments began as loans, the Company came to be the registered owner of substantial percentages of the New England textile firms, presumably the result of defaulted loans. "In no cross-section year did that institution hold less than $80,000 in stock in the eleven companies, and in 1854 the holdings totaled $390,500."[28] Thus, the Massachusetts Hospital Life Insurance Company, both as lender and later as owner/trustee, provided control and opportunity to Boston society and by extension to Massachusetts industry.

Another important factor in the development of the textile firms as it relates to trusts and trusteeships was the organization of the textile businesses as corporations and not as partnerships. "British textile firms and the smaller American concerns established up to then were, with few exceptions, organized as individual proprietorships or partnerships."[29] When Lowell, Nathan Appleton and other Boston Associates formed the Boston Manufacturing Company, they incorporated the business rather than forming a partnership.[30] The Boston Manufacturing Company has been described as "the original American corporation."[31] Lowell solicited eleven men to raise capital. Each bought shares that then enabled a new type of organization with share transferability (by sale, gift, or transfer to trusts) and infinite duration. Unlike a partnership, corporations, whose shares could be transferred or sold, provided a potential exit strategy and liquidity to a shareholder. This was a critical consideration to the original investors in these risky textile ventures.[32]

From 1809 until 1830, Massachusetts law did not limit shareholder liability for corporate debts. Prior to 1830, "[i]t was, therefore, necessary for the investor to watch carefully the management of his company and the prospects of its success."[33] Because 1821 through 1828 were years of prosperity, unlimited liability did not appear to present a great danger to the shareholders. However, corporate failures in 1829 changed that view.[34] In 1830, the Massachusetts legislature reacted to the petitions of corporate manufacturing company shareholders to enact a law limiting liability of the shareholder.[35] This allowed potential investors and, most importantly for our purposes, trustees to invest in companies without putting other trust assets at risk.

The ability of Massachusetts trustees to legally[36] invest in company stock and with limited liability after 1830 allowed their trusts to invest in one of the great economic booms of the time – the textile industry. It also allowed the Boston Associates to use trusts to control ownership of their precious shares. The proof of this is found in the shifting percentage of ownership of these shares from individuals to trusts over time. In 1834, merchants owned 39.3% of the equity of New England textile firms and trustees owned 4.1%. By 1859, these figures had moved to 24.8% and 16.6%, an almost one-to-one shift from individual ownership to trust ownership.[37] We can attribute this to two factors: (1) the death of some of the original investors, who left their shares in trust for their families; and (2) the purchase of shares by other trustees, presumably because they viewed investing in the shares as a safe and profitable investment.[38] As the Massachusetts Hospital Life Insurance Company initially could not directly own these shares, trusts with individual trustees were the Boston Associates' only option for post-death control over their shares.

While the corporate form today often results in a wider group of owners than other business structures, that was not true of the early Massachusetts textile companies. For example, Francis Cabot Lowell, an original shareholder of the Boston Manufacturing Company, was related to five other subscribers through marriage. "By 1820 there were thirteen additional subscribers to the stock of the Boston Manufacturing Co., but the kinship connections of several of the individuals to the Lowells and Jacksons ensured that the original subscribers retained majority control in the company."[39] By 1845, the Boston Associates comprised about eighty men who controlled about one-fifth of the capacity of the American cotton spinning industry.[40] Their interrelationships and control over much of the Massachusetts economy can be inferred from this fact; that in 1848 seventeen of these men served as directors of seven Boston banks, holding over 40% of the city's authorized banking capital.[41]

This tight control did not benefit everyone. In 1863, a pamphlet attacking the control of the textile companies and the overreaching by the Massachusetts Hospital Life Insurance Company declared:

> From a clique of twelve or fifteen men in Boston, Directors enough are taken to make a majority of each board in most of the great manufacturing companies of the State . . . .

This clique are almost all associates or officers of the Massachusetts Hospital Life Insurance Company.[42]

The complaints directed towards the Boston Associates and trustee control of Boston's finances continued, including a 1933 *Fortune* magazine article that complained:

How much money has been so retired out to stud there is, of course, no means of telling. The trustees are numerous and impossible to access. Hardly a Boston family of any size but has one or two members who act as trustees, active or inactive, under some uncle's will, while most law offices have a partner or two to undertake the same work officially and the banks have the usual trust departments.[43]

These economic ties combined with social and family ties to create a very tight closed society, and one that contrasted distinctly with those found elsewhere. "Although Philadelphia and New York were both larger and richer, enjoying incalculably greater access to the natural resources and interior markets essential to economic growth, their sharp religious divisions and imperfect legal architecture hampered the capacity of their elites to pool their resources for either economic or institutional purposes."[44]

The explosive economic growth created by the successive economic booms of shipping and then textiles marked the financial takeoff point for the families that would eventually constitute the core of Boston's "Brahmin" elite. This emergent upper class was "recognized as subtly different from the 'society' of other cities. The Boston aristocracy was famous for gentility and wealth, for its frugality, temperance, dynasticism, its hostility to ostentation and waste. The upper classes were characterized by strong 'family' consciousness, and a sense of historical tradition."[45]

Not only were the Boston families tied together economically, with a small group of men running the mills, banks, and other growth engines, they even lived together in close proximity. In the middle of the nineteenth century, Boston was much smaller geographically than it is today. Water bounded the Boston Common to the west (what is now known as the Back Bay was under water) and State Street was hundreds of feet shorter than it is now. Significantly, all forty-one men in Boston worth between $500,000 and $3,000,000[46] in 1851 lived within blocks of one another:

> Summer Street was the home of the Sam Gardner family; Lees, Jacksons, and Putnams, all related to each other, congregated about Chauncy Place and Bedford Street; Perkinses in Temple Place; Lawrences and Masons in the part of Tremont Street between West and Boylston, then called Colonnade Row; Eliots in Park and Beacon; Amorys in Franklin Street (then such a pretty place with a little grass park down the middle); the head of the Sears family lived in the house of the Somerset Club . . . and their married children lived on each side; Curtises and Lorings were in Somerset Street.[47]

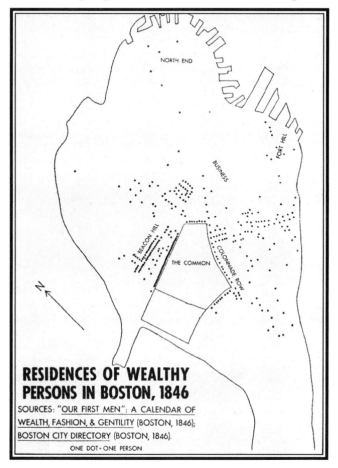

FIREY MAP OF BOSTON WEALTHY

Boston families not only did business together and lived together, they intermarried with remarkable frequency, further creating bonds and control in a small group of families: "In Boston . . . families whose stay in America had been relatively brief but whose wealth was great, established intimate ties with the city's patriciate."[48] According to one typical description of the intermarriages, "[Y]oung women of the great Amory family married Lorings, Sohiers, Dexters, Eckleys, Prescotts . . . Codmans, Lowells, and Appletons, while male Amorys gave their names to wives of the Greene, Sargent, Codman, and Sears families."[49] And, of course, Ann Amory married John McLean.

The Revolutionary War created a vacuum in leadership when many upper class loyalists returned to England or departed for other locales. The newly wealthy merchants and manufacturers stepped into this void to create a new upper class with its own culture and dynamics. The rapid evolution and investment of their wealth into corporate stock in corporations created an enormous pool of assets. Their desire to protect their families and preserve this wealth made trusts exceedingly useful, and using Boston Trustees (trusted members of their own social class), seemed both reassuring and prudent. As we will see in the next chapter, trusts also provided a means of stable ownership, without which the growth of these new corporations would almost cetainly have been inhibited.

The Beneficiary:
Control and Care

When parents dye intestate, the Elder sonne shall have
a doble portion of his whole estate reall and personal,
unlesse the Generall Court upon just cause alleaged
shall Judge otherwise.[1]

T HE BENEFICIARY is the person the trust property is supposed to benefit. Trusts are created to protect people or to protect property. Trusts can protect people from themselves if they are spendthrifts or need special care and can protect them from third parties in case of divorce or fraud. Often, trusts are used to protect property from the decisions of the beneficiaries and from the government's taxes.

The United States estate tax was not put into place until 1916.

Before that, inheritances were taxed only
moderately by a few individual states, whereby
those taxes were often nonprogressive, the tax
rates of most states were below 10%, and only
the inheritances of collateral relatives were
taxed. On the federal level, inheritances were
taxed only three times in the nineteenth
century; in each instance it was war-related and
did not last very long....[2]

The federal estate tax signed into law by Woodrow
Wilson in late 1916 ranged from 1% for a taxable estate of less than $50,000 to 10% for an estate over
$5,000,000. The first $50,000 was tax exempt.[3]
Once imposed, the federal estate tax, with marginal
rates of as high as 77% during one period, became a
major driver of trust usage in the United States.

Under current U.S. law, trusts can be structured
to be separate entities for income tax purposes. In
times of high income tax rates and large steps in
marginal rates, trusts have been used to minimize
income taxes on family wealth. In addition, trusts
can be structured to keep the trust property out of
beneficiaries' estates, thereby avoiding estate taxes,
possibly for generations. Even if the impetus for
placing property in trust is initially "only" to minimize or eliminate taxes, the resulting trusts are still
real, requiring competent trusteeship to carefully
manage all normal trust issues and requirements.

Where one beneficiary is supposed to benefit from
property for a limited time and then the donor wishes to ensure that whatever is left over passes to the
next person by law, a trust provides the ideal vehicle
to fulfill that desire. Ann McLean was to benefit
from the income from $50,000, but whatever was

left over was specifically guaranteed to pass to Harvard College and the Massachusetts General Hospital, not to any second spouse Ann might have had or to other charities in which she might have had an interest.

The corporate form of business ownership also offered many favorable estate planning attributes for Boston society. For example, unlike a partnership where the death of a partner tied up the business during probate, a corporation could continue to operate despite the death of an owner with no delay for settling the estate. Corporate form alone, however, could not solve all of the inheritance problems for Bostonians.

One important problem that remained was that the laws of inheritance forced the splintering of interests upon death unless proper planning was undertaken. Under English law in the late seventeenth and early eighteenth centuries, the eldest son inherited the entire estate, a system called primogeniture. The Puritan founders of the Massachusetts Bay and the Plymouth Colonies deliberately rejected this English inheritance system, favoring instead one called "partible inheritance." Under partible inheritance, each child received an equal share of the decedent's estate subject to the rights of the surviving spouse. Massachusetts partible inheritance also provided for equal treatment of male and female descendants.[4] In 1733, in *Philips v. Savage*,[5] the Suffolk County Court and later the Privy Council affirmed the use of partible inheritance in Massachusetts despite its deviance from English law.[6] The early Massachusetts version of partible inheritance provided for the eldest son to receive a double share in comparison to his siblings, but this extra share provision was abolished in 1789.[7]

Partible inheritance meant that each share of stock in a corporation like the Boston Manufacturing Company might have been transferred under the will of the older generation free of trust to multiple inheritors, splintering at each generation. Thus, at each division, the shares of a textile company would have been held by more and more people, not all of whom would be equally wise or capable of making the best decisions for the business's livelihood and future. New shareholders might have intefered with the company's business or might have decided to sell their shares, actions that could have proven disruptive. As Oliver Wendell Holmes wrote in 1859, "Of course, this trivial and fugitive fact of personal wealth does not create a permanent class, unless some special means are taken to arrest the process of disintegration in the third generation."[8] To avoid this "disintegration," some corporations, like the Massachusetts Hospital Life Insurance Company, required shares to be sold back to the directors, who could then control to whom they would be resold.[9]

The solution for many of the Boston Associates was to leave their shares in trust at death. Depending upon the terms of the trust, this allowed beneficiaries to receive the income from the shares, but allowed the trust's donor to ensure that the trust property was managed correctly and did not dissipate. A trust could outlive several generations, thus limiting the times that the share holding would be forced to "splinter."

Harvard College and the Massachusetts General Hospital sued the trustees of the trust for Ann McLean over the value and reasonableness of holding the shares of the Boston Manufacturing Company and the Merrimack Manufacturing Company in trust, which was precisely the type of situation feared by the men using corporations and trusts to further their economic interests. The Court's decision to uphold the trustees' retention of the shares confirmed the use of trusts to hold and preserve corporate ownership. It assured Boston society that the death of the original merchants would not result in the dissolution of their capital through division or poor management. We will discuss the case in more depth in a later chapter.

The Law

*There is undoubtedly, in the execution of most trusts, much
solicitude and vexation, which cannot be compensated by
money; and any trustee must be supposed to understand
this, when he takes upon himself such a burden.*[1]

THE POST-WAR of 1812 Boston economy
gave rise to a social and business class rich
enough to be interested in trusts and to
support a trust "business." During the same time
period, the Massachusetts legal backdrop for trusts
also changed in a very favorable direction. The trust
law of other states also developed at this time, but
the law of trust investment took two distinct paths,
with Massachusetts adopting laws and developing
case law favorable to individual professional trustees and other states not moving in that direction as
smoothly or as rapidly.

Neither a trustee nor the beneficiaries have complete ownership of a trust. The trustee holds legal title to the trust property, but he does so for the benefit of the beneficiaries. The beneficiary has an equitable claim to the benefit of the property, but does not own the assets. Historically, this split of ownership did not fit the type of case found in a typical court of law and thus, in England, trusts were only enforceable in special courts. These special courts were called courts of equity, and their rulings were based upon "equity jurisdiction." Unfortunately, English courts of equity, especially the Star Chamber, came to have a very poor reputation, particularly in America where they were seen as examples of English persecution of the Puritans.[2]

Insecurity over court power led the Massachusetts Constitution of 1780 to deny the courts of the Commonwealth equity jurisdiction. Instead, equity power was reserved to the Massachusetts Legislature, leaving trustees and trust beneficiaries to petition the Legislature for remedies to their disagreements. This was an inefficient process and it was essential to the development of Massachusetts trust practice that equity powers be made available to the courts.

Despite a lack of jurisdiction, some trust cases were brought before the Massachusetts Supreme Judicial Court, but in those cases, the Court either refused to rule or interpreted its powers as narrowly as possible.[3] For example, in 1804, the Massachusetts Supreme Judicial Court declined to enforce a trust created under a will on the grounds that the Court lacked equity jurisdiction, stating: "[I]f the conveyance was in *trust*, this Court could not have compelled the execution of it; and, until the legislature shall think it proper to give us further powers, we can do nothing upon subjects of *that* nature."[4]

It was Joseph Story who almost singlehandedly brought equity jurisdiction to the Massachusetts courts.[5] Story was born in Marblehead in 1779. His father had taken part in the Boston Tea Party in 1773. He graduated from Harvard College, passed the bar in 1801, and read law with Samuel Putnam, who would later craft the Prudent Man Rule. In 1805, he was elected to the Massachusetts House of Representatives and in 1808 to the United States Congress. At the age of thirty-two, Story was named to the United States Supreme Court where he served until 1845.

In 1808, while still a member of the Massachusetts House of Representatives, the state legislature appointed Story to deliver a report on the subject of equity jurisdiction for the courts. A committee was formed and a bill drafted that would have given full equity powers to the courts. Despite all of Story's efforts, this bill was defeated. Story continued to apply pressure on the Legislature, but instead of granting the courts full equity powers in one piece of legislation, the Legislature granted the courts equity powers topic by topic. In February of 1817, the Supreme Judicial Court was given equity powers with respect to trusts.[6] With this new power, the Court began to establish the essential tenets of trusts and trusteeship that would allow for certainty in legal practice and provide settled law in the field.

Under its new equity power, rulings on five legal principles by the court were essential to a favorable environment for trusts and the use of individual professional trustees in Massachusetts.[7] First was the establishment of the Rule Against Perpetuities, which allowed settlors of trusts to put large sums of money into professional hands and remove it from

The Law

the risks of divorce and wasting behavior for approximately one hundred years. Second was the enforcement of "spendthrift clauses," which prevented a beneficiary's creditors from reaching the trust property to settle his or her debts. Third was court approval of the ability of trustees to receive reasonable compensation. Fourth was court recognition of circumstances where the rights and powers of the donor and trustees could trump those of the beneficiaries. Finally, and most importantly, the establishment of a liberal investment standard that was flexible over time for trustees, allowed both individual trustees and corporate trustees to invest without the threat of debilitating lawsuits. This final aspect is of such significance that we will explore it in its own chapter.

RULE AGAINST PERPETUITIES. In 1833, the Massachusetts Supreme Judicial Court, through Chief Justice Lemuel Shaw, established the Rule Against Perpetuities for Massachusetts.[8] The Rule provides that interests in trust are void unless they must vest within the lifetimes of persons alive at the creation of the trust, plus twenty-one years. Determining when an interest is "vested" is not always easy and can depend upon arcane legal rules. For our purposes, the Rule is a legal limitation on the duration of a non-charitable trust to approximately one hundred years. Of course, the corollary of the limit was that within the limit, trusts could be used and had the protection of the law. For example, if the donor's grandchild was one year old when the trust was established and died at age eighty, the trust could last for 100 years (79 years of the grandchild's life, plus 21 years).

[73]

The Rule Against Perpetuities strikes a balance between the desire of the trust's donor to protect and control the funds of his beneficiaries for as long as possible with the public policy of limiting long-term or indefinite restraints on transfers of property. Without a termination date for a trust, the increasing numbers of beneficiaries at each generation would eventually splinter the trust's interests to the point where it would become both administratively onerous and beneficially worthless. In 2012, Professor Lawrence Waggoner argued against interminable trusts, noting that under current actuarial assumptions after 250 years a trust will have more than 7,000 living beneficiaries.[9] While the legal prevention of trusts of infinite duration may have frustrated the intent of some donors, the same result seems to have been achieved in Boston informally, for by the early twentieth century it had become common for a beneficiary who received terminating distributions from long-term trusts to turn around and again place the property into a new long-term trust:

> It was and is the accepted practice for the young Forbes or Lowell whom the Rule Against Perpetuities could make outright owner of several millions of gilt-edged bonds to reëstablish voluntarily his family trust. And failing the voluntary act there are always enough aunts and uncles and trustees to see that the deed in any case is done.[10]

CREDITOR PROTECTION: THE SPENDTHRIFT CLAUSE. If trusts were to be truly useful as control vehicles, they needed to be protected from the reach of the beneficiaries' creditors. The effectiveness of a statement in a trust preventing a beneficiary's creditors from reaching the trust property (a so-called "spendthrift clause") was finally established in Massachusetts in the 1882 Massachusetts Supreme Judicial Court case of *Broadway National Bank v. Adams*.[11] However, several closely related questions had been addressed by Massachusetts courts previously and were probably sufficient to reassure donors that trusts could protect their family's assets from creditors.[12] In the 1824 case of *Braman v. Stiles*, the will of a father left the property of one of his sons in the hands of the other two "for his comfort and advantage, according to their best judgment and discretion."[13] The son's creditors sought to reach the son's share of the father's estate. Chief Justice Parker held:

> [F]or he having the power of disposing of his property as he pleased, had a right to prevent it from going to the creditors of his son, or from being wasted by the son himself, if, as was probable, he had become incapable of taking care of property. Creditors have no right to complain; for unless such disposition can be made, without doubt testators, in like situations would give their property to their other children.[14]

In the same year, in *Russell v. Lewis*, the Massachusetts Supreme Judicial Court professed not to have the power in equity to reach trust assets for a debt of the beneficiary, claiming,

> [I]t is certain that we have no statute making trust estates chargeable with the debts of the *cestui que trust*; and as they are not so

chargeable by the principles of the common law, we are brought to the conclusion, that the tenant acquired no title by extending his execution against [the trustee] on the premises.[15]

In *Perkins v. Hays*, the Court held that a beneficiary could not pledge a portion of an annuity in anticipation of its receipt, thus both protecting the beneficiary and preserving discretionary trustee power over the distribution of trust income and principal.[16]

TRUSTEE COMPENSATION. In addition to a basis for enforcing trusts in equity and the enforcement of spendthrift provisions, a true trusteeship profession required the certainty of reasonable compensation. Beginning with English rules of equity, charging for trustee services was seen as creating an inherent conflict of interest that should be avoided. When one thinks of engaging in the duty of administering property for others without compensation, but with possible liability, the problem becomes obvious:

It comes to this: "Will you be so kind as to undertake the management of my affairs and my family's for an indefinite period – to bestow more pains and care upon them than I should myself, at the risk of being answerable – and no quarter given – for the slightest indiscretion, and do all this for nothing?" Stated thus – and not over-stated – the coolness of the proposal becomes apparent: yet do settlors or testators ever realize this? Do they even manifest any gratitude? Not one in a hundred.[17]

The ability of a trustee to charge for his services in

Massachusetts was made clear in 1819 when Chief
Justice Parker held:

> [I]n *England* trustees are generally allowed
> nothing; and the same rule is applied to
> executors, who are considered as voluntarily
> accepting the trust. In this commonwealth,
> however, executors are allowed a reasonable
> compensation; and there is no reason why
> trustees should not be. Indeed it will probably
> be for the advantage of all, who are concerned
> in estates held in trust, that such compensation
> should be made; as more care and diligence
> may be expected and required, where there is a
> compensation.[18]

It is interesting to note that the strict enforcement of
the English law was not in fact the practice for many
trustees in England as the grantor could, under
English law, make provisions in his will for trustee
compensation or for a bequest to his trustee. In fact,
"[b]y the close of Victoria's reign it had almost become the rule."[19]

The early allowance of compensation for trustees
in Massachusetts was an exception to the general
rule for other jurisdictions. In New York, for example, while a statute was enacted in 1817 allowing
compensation to executors, trustee compensation
was only allowed on a case-by-case basis. It was not
until 1866 that an Act was passed that expressly provided that trustees were entitled to the same compensation as executors.[20]

Some early professional trustees charged by having fee provisions placed in the trust document either expressly or disguised as bequests. The early

rate appears to have been 5% of the trust's annual income.[21] There are indications that the normal rate increased to 6% of income after the imposition of the federal income tax in 1913.[22] In most cases, trustees are now entitled to "reasonable compensation," although some states still have statutory fee schedules.[23]

The trend in Massachusetts has been to de-emphasize fees on income and instead adopt the principal-oriented approach of investment advisors, with fees hovering around 1% of the trust assets annually with the rate declining as the size of the trust increases. For many years in Boston, trustees charged based upon a percentage of the income earned annually in the trust plus a percentage of the principal, with the total fee aggregating close to the asset-based fee. An example of such a schedule would be:

SCHEDULE OF FEES

Principal

First. $1,000,000....0.75%
Next. $4,000,000....0.35%
Next. $10,000,000....0.20%
Above. $15,000,000....0.10%

Income

6% of income collected

This fee schedule would result in an annual fee of $19,900 on a $3 million trust with interest and dividends of $90,000. This is a fee of .663% or about two-thirds of 1%.

Although the Proposals of the Massachusetts Hospital Life Insurance Company touted that they would charge lower rates than the private trustees of the time,[24] current rate schedules of large national corporate trustees usually exceed those of the Boston Trustee firms.

DONOR AND TRUSTEE POWER. As we have seen, Massachusetts law for trustees and donors seeking to control property in trust changed favorably through the early 1800s. Some have implied that this path of change was a directed, planned, and organized change to the law spearheaded by the Boston Associates in an effort to control their families and fortunes.[25] While changes to Massachusetts case law certainly helped the Boston Associates maintain their wealth in trust and were a precursor to the rise of the individual professional trustee, it seems an overstatement to attribute a master plan to the development. However, no case better enforced the impression that the judges were helping trustees and donors to control property and to keep it out of the hands of beneficiaries than the 1868 Massachusetts case of *Minot v. Paine.*[26] In *Minot*, the question was raised whether a trustee (William Minot, Jr.) should allocate stock dividends (as opposed to cash dividends) to income and pay them out to the beneficiaries or should allocate them to principal and retain them in the trust. Chief Justice Chapman, in announcing what came to be called the "Rule in Minot's Case," held that "a stock dividend is an accretion to his capital; and there is nothing to show that the testator intended that it should be otherwise in between successive takers of his bounty."[27] The result was to allow individual trustees, who were often also directors of the companies in which they invested, both to declare and retain in trust a stock dividend they would otherwise have had to distribute had it been declared as a cash dividend.

Chapman's holding created a firestorm of controversy in Boston society as beneficiaries worried that trustees would limit their income by declaring dividends in stock rather than cash, thereby making those dividends trust principal. A book was written at the time ridiculing the decision and even featuring a poem by John Sargent Osborne likening the Justice's reasoning to that of someone residing in the Massachusetts mental hospital (which we will see was named after John McLean).[28]

> "Study this case, sir (and it's well worth
> studying) and you'll find that income is capital,
> earnings are capital, dividends are capital,
> allotted shares are capital, distributions are
> capital – and indeed sir, I challenge you to find
> any word in the language that is intended to
> apply to the proceeds of capital, that under
> this decision may not mean capital, and
> nothing else."[29]

While the *Minot* decision can be seen as an example of the courts favoring trustees over beneficiaries, the 1889 case of *Claflin v. Claflin*[30] is an example of the courts' giving priority to the wishes of the donor that property remain in trust over the wishes of the beneficiaries to have property distributed. In *Claflin*, the testator created a trust for his son. The terms of the trust provided that the son would receive $10,000 when he reached age 21, $10,000 at age 25 and the balance of the trust when he reached age 30. After receiving his first $10,000 at age 21 and prior to attaining age 25, the son brought an action to compel the trustees to pay him the remainder of the trust, contending that the trust provisions postponing distribution beyond age 21 were void. Interestingly, the trust did not contain a spendthrift provision. The Court refused to dissolve the trust despite it being fully vested:

> This is not a dry trust, nor have the purposes of the trust been accomplished, if the intention of the testator is to be carried out....

> It cannot be said that these restrictions upon the plaintiff's possession and control of the property are altogether useless, for there is not the same danger that he will spend the property while it is in the hands of the trustees as there would be if it were in his own.[31]

The courts' holdings supporting trustee and donor control over the trusts, provided additional reassurance to Boston families wishing to place their wealth in trust.

The favorable legal foundation for trusts and professional trustees created by Massachusetts courts in the 1800s was critical to the rise of the Boston Trustee. Without equity jurisdiction, trustees could not easily rectify or resolve disputes. Without the Rule Against Perpetuities, long-term control might have been thwarted or state law would have interfered to further limit the duration of trusts. Without protection against creditors, trusts would have been much more vulnerable and less useful to Boston society. Without routine trustee compensation, being a trustee could not have developed into a true profession of specialists. Finally, without cases favoring trustee powers and a preference for maintaining trusts, the actual use of trusts would have been less advantageous. The unique legal backdrop of trust case law in Massachusetts was inseparable from the creation and subsequent development of the Boston Trustee.

Trust Investments

*In the ninth volume of Pickering's Reports . . . is a report of
the suit brought by Harvard College and the Hospital . . . in
which the Court decided that the Trustees had the right to
select any stocks they pleased for the trust-fund.*[1]

W HEN McLEAN DIED, about one-half of
his estate was made up of shares in the
Boston Manufacturing Company and
the Merrimack Manufacturing Company. The executors of the estate funded the $50,000 trust for
Mrs. McLean with 9 shares of each company which
were stated in their account as together being worth
$25,200 of the initial $50,000. The rest of the fund
was made up of 78 shares of bank stock and 247
shares of "F. and Marine Insurance Co." The Trustees of Ann's trust were permitted by the terms of the
trust to "loan the same upon ample and sufficient

security, or to invest the same in safe and productive stock, either in the public funds, bank shares or other stock, according to their best judgment and discretion."[2]

Harvard College and the Hospital, the remainder beneficiaries, negotiated with the trustees over the trust, offering to pay Mrs. McLean a six percent $3,000 annual annuity in exchange for delivery by the trustees of the assets to the charities outright. We do not know if there was a particular reason why the institutions were not satisfied with the trustees managing the trust. The negotiations failed to produce a compromise, and the assets were placed in the trust. The trustees wrote to the charities: "It is plain to us that our Testator had great confidence in the stocks, and that he intended that his wife should enjoy her fair share of all income and profits of his estate."[3]

The account setting forth the funding of the trust was not objected to by Harvard and, while the Hospital made some objections, they were denied and the account was approved by the probate court. In August of 1828, Jonathan Amory died and was not replaced as trustee. Later, in October of that year, when Francis Amory, the surviving trustee, tendered his resignation and presented the accounts of his trusteeship to the probate court for allowance, the charities sought to surcharge him for declines in the value of the insurance and manufacturing stocks on the ground that they were not proper trust investments. The beneficiaries did not challenge the concentration of the trust investments in so few securities as they would have today. The probate court approved Amory's account and the charities appealed to the Massachusetts Supreme Judicial Court.[4]

SAMUEL PUTNAM

The decision that followed, *Harvard College v. Amory*, provided trustees in Massachusetts with a standard of conduct for the investment of trust funds that was very flexible.[5] The Court tied the standard to current practice in the community, making it self-adjusting for changes in investment practice over time. This holding is today most commonly referred to as the "Prudent Man Rule." This legal recipe for investing was missing in other states and this factor, more than any other, helps explain the advancement and success of trusts and the role the Boston Trustee plays in Massachusetts alone.

The decision of the Court was written by Justice Samuel Putnam. Putnam was born in 1768 in Danvers, Massachusetts, attended Harvard College and studied law in Salem where he became a prominent lawyer. He served in the Massachusetts Legislature in the House and the Senate from 1808 until 1814, when Governor Strong named him to the Massachusetts Supreme Judicial Court upon the death of Chief Justice Samuel Sewall. Putnam served on the Court for twenty-eight years. He was well-connected, well-respected and well-liked.[6] "Members of the bar join with his compeers on the bench to declare that no opinions or judgments of a high tribunal were ever more likely to be sound, sober, practical, and to the point, than his, as they are recorded on the books."[7] Although Putnam was well connected to Brahmin society, his social connections were not thought to have affected his judgment. "If his personal friends were interested in a case, they feared that, in his jealous impartiality, he would rather lean against them than in their behalf."[8] Nathaniel I. Bowditch, the son of the Navigator, who is quoted criticizing the holding of the *Harvard College v. Amory* case at the beginning of this chapter, ironically sent Putnam a copy of his history of the Massachusetts General Hospital containing his criticism. Putnam wrote to Bowditch praising the book and thanking his *friend* for the gift.[9]

With only a small change in timing, Putnam would have been conflicted out of being able to sit on the case and we might not have the Prudent Man Rule. When Jonathan Amory, trustee of the McLean trust, died in August of 1828, no successor for the McLean trust was appointed and Francis Amory was left as the sole remaining trustee of the trust. However, after the *Harvard College v. Amory* case, when Ann McLean's nephew, John Amory Lowell, was appointed as sole trustee to replace Francis

Amory, the charities objected, claiming that two trustees were required. John Amory Lowell, a prominent Brahmin, was the Treasurer of the Merrimack Manufacturing Company from 1827 until 1844 and would later become its President. Putnam was conflicted out of the case over the appointment of two trustees, as Lowell had married Putnam's daughter on April 9, 1829.[10] If the charities had objected to having a single trustee in 1828 when Jonathan had died and Lowell had been appointed then, Putnam would have been blocked from sitting on the investment case when it was heard in 1830.

Even without a direct conflict, it is clear that Putnam was very well connected to the Boston Associates through family relationships.

> When John Amory Lowell married for the
> second time in 1829 after the death of Susan
> Lowell, it was to Elizabeth Cabot Putnam
> (1809–1881), daughter of Judge Samuel Putnam
> of Salem. One of Elizabeth (Putnam) Lowell's
> brothers, Samuel R. Putnam (1797–1861),
> married Mary Trail Spence Lowell (1810–1898),
> another first cousin of John Amory Lowell,
> thus doubly establishing the Putnam
> connection to the Lowell kin network in this
> cohort."[11]

Putnam would later become the father-in-law of Charles Greeley Loring, another well-connected Brahmin with a trusteeship practice. Thus, it is certain he was familiar with, and likely predisposed to, Boston Trustees and their investment preferences.

The lawyers who represented the two sides in the case are prime examples of the closeness of Boston society of the time. Samuel Hubbard represented the charities. Hubbard had practiced law with Charles Jackson who left the practice in 1813 to become a Supreme Judicial Court Justice.[12] A very successful lawyer, he was the first solicitor of the Massachusetts Hospital Life Insurance Company and was one of its original directors.[13] Hubbard himself became a Supreme Judicial Court Justice in 1842, actually replacing Putnam.[14] Among the lawyers representing the McLean trustee, Francis Amory, was Lemuel Shaw, who witnessed the will itself and perhaps drafted it. Shaw himself was appointed to the Supreme Judicial Court on August 30, 1830, five months after this case was decided. Shaw and Putnam became great friends and mutual admirers.[15]

In their argument against the trust investments, the charities cited a case called *Trafford v. Boehm* that had, not surprisingly, held with the benefit of hindsight that the stock of the South Sea Company was not a proper trust investment.[16] The Company had been founded in a scheme to reduce the size of England's public debt. In exchange for absorbing a large portion of the debt, the Company received exclusive rights to trade with South America. Stock in the South Sea Company had been manipulated and risen quickly to bubble levels before famously collapsing in 1720. The charities urged the Court to adopt the so-called "English rule" with respect to trustee investments. Under that rule, only government securities and well-secured first mortgages qualified as proper trust investments. Putnam summarized the English rule to limit investment in "funds or other good securities. . . such as have the engagement of the government to pay off their capital."[17]

Putnam, speaking for the Court, rejected the English rule as having very little or no application to American trust law because securities meeting that standard were both exceedingly limited in amount compared to the extent of the trust funds available to invest and, in any event, were not necessarily safe investments. "It is said that the public policy in England of compelling trustees to invest trust funds in government funds originated largely in the necessities of the government, and the public advantage of creating a market and demand for government securities."[18] Putnam was aware of the United States government's default on interest payments on government debt on November 9, 1814 (during the War of 1812).

Putnam's decision as to the sustainability of the investments in corporate stock was influenced by McLean's reputation as a prudent investor himself:

> In the case at bar, the testator was a man of extraordinary forecast and discretion, in regard to the management of his property. His vast accumulation could not be ascribed to accidental causes, but to calculation and reflection. The fact that he had within three or four years invested nearly half of his property in manufacturing stock, was entitled to great consideration and respect, and would, without any change of circumstances, have a strong tendency to justify the selection of the manufacturing stock as part of the trust fund."[19]

The essence of this notable ruling, which has come to be called the Prudent Man Rule, was as follows:

> All that can be required of a trustee to invest,

is, that he shall conduct himself faithfully and exercise a sound discretion. He is to observe how men of prudence, discretion and intelligence manage their own affairs, not in regard to speculation, but in regard to the permanent disposition of their funds, considering the probable income, as well as the probable safety of the capital to be invested.[20]

The Prudent Man Rule therefore is a rule that defines trustee conduct, rather than one that demands performance.[21] Under the Rule, trustees are not insurers and are not required to guarantee investment results. If a trustee has conducted himself properly, then a decline in the value of a trust asset is not, in and of itself, grounds for surcharge. Although the Court decided the case in favor of the trustees primarily on procedural grounds, the Court made it clear that it would have decided the case in their favor in any event because the trustees' investing conduct was proper.

The ability of Massachusetts trustees to invest in textile company stock and other stock available at the time allowed Massachusetts trusts to benefit from the huge appreciation in the income and value of those companies. In turn, the Boston Associates were allowed to use trusts to control ownership of those companies for generations. Both were central factors allowing Boston Trustees to flourish.

NEW YORK LAW. As important as the *Harvard College v. Amory* decision was to the development of Massachusetts trusteeship, the lack of facilitating investment discretion law in other jurisdictions prevented its growth elsewhere. For example, thirty-nine years after the *Harvard College* decision, the New York Supreme Court in *King v. Talbot*[22] took a similar standard for the review of trust investments and came to an entirely different conclusion. In that case, Justice Woodruff announced a standard that is remarkably similar to the one set forth in *Harvard College*:

> My own judgment, after an examination of the subject, and bearing in mind the nature of the office, its importance, and the considerations, which alone induce men of suitable experience, capacity, and responsibility to accept its usually thankless burden, is, that the just and true rule is, that the trustee is bound to employ such diligence and such prudence in the care and management, as in general, prudent men of discretion and intelligence in such matters, employ in their own like affairs.[23]

However, the Court then took a conservative view of trust investments that affected New York trustees for many years:

> This necessarily excludes all speculation, all investments for an uncertain and doubtful rise in the market, and, of course, everything that does not take into view the nature and object of the trust, and the consequences of a mistake in the selection of the investment to be made.

> It, therefore, does not follow, that, because prudent men may, and often do, conduct their own affairs with the hope of growing rich, and therein take the hazard of adventures which

they deem hopeful, trustees may do the same; the preservation of the fund, and the procurement of a just income therefrom, are primary objects of the creation of the trust itself, and are to be primarily regarded.[24]

According to the New York Court, the preservation of capital and the avoidance of risk of loss was the primary duty of a trustee:

> The moment the fund is invested in bank, or insurance, or railroad stock, it has left the control of the trustees; its safety and the hazard, or risk of loss, is no longer dependent upon their skill, care, or discretion, in its custody or management, and the terms of the investment do not contemplate that it will ever be returned to the trustees.[25]

The Court therefore found stock in any corporation not to be a prudent investment as if it were the equivalent of directly buying a business. Trustees at that time would not be authorized to directly hold businesses in trust absent extraordinary circumstances. It is interesting to note that New York, without a strong tradition of private trustees, gave broader investment discretion to corporate trustees than to individuals, and that discrepancy was not eliminated until 1914.[26]

PENNSYLVANIA LAW. Pennsylvania followed the English rule of *Trafford v. Boehm*[27] to severely restrict the ability of trustees to invest.[28] At the time of *Harvard College v. Amory*, in 1832 the Pennsylvania Legislature passed a statute governing trustee investing, providing that a trustee:

> [M]ay present a petition to the Orphans' Court
> of the proper county, stating the circum-
> stances of the case, and the amount or sum of
> money which he is desirous of investing; where
> upon, it shall be lawful for the court, upon due
> proof, to make an order directing the
> investment of such moneys in the stock or
> public debt of the United States, or in the public
> debt of this commonwealth, or in the public
> debt of the city of Philadelphia, or on real
> securities, at such prices or on such rates of
> interest and terms of payment respectively
> as the court shall think fit; and in case the said
> monies shall be invested conformably to such
> directions, the said.... trustee, shall be exempt
> ed from all liability for loss on the same.... [28]

The Pennsylvania courts enforced these rules to
hold fiduciaries liable who strayed from the legally
allowed list. In *Hemphill's Appeal*, the court made it
clear that any variation from the procedure of court
authorization would strip the trustee of liability protection:

> There is no reason why the trustee should not
> make the investment in some security which
> cannot fail. It is just as convenient. In the country
> real security can always be had; and in the
> cities and large towns, there is no trouble about
> getting government stocks. It is better for
> trustees that the rule of their conduct should be
> clearly defined and well understood. A plain path,
> though it may be a narrow one, is safer to walk

in than a trackless waste, where no man can
be sure he is on the right course.[29]

Putnam understood that an investor has to take on
risk to have a chance at a higher than risk-free return. Here we can see the stark difference between
Putnam's realistic understanding of investments,
"Do what you will, the capital is at hazard,"[30] and the
unrealistic expectation of the Pennsylvania court.

In 1873, Pennsylvania's new Constitution forbade
trustees from investing in stock: "[n]o act of the
general assembly shall authorize the investment of
trust funds by executors, administrators, guard-
ians or other trustees, in the bonds or stock of any
private corporation, and such acts now existing are
avoided saving investments heretofore made."[31] This
remained the law in Pennsylvania until 1933.

OTHER STATES. In 1831, Maryland gave the Or-
phans Court the right to order any administrator or
guardian to invest as it directed.[32] Alabama, Colora-
do, Montana and Wyoming all had similar statutes
that limited the investment discretion of trustees.[33]

Whether one thinks that the Massachusetts rule
is good or bad will depend upon the identity of the
trustee and whether one fears mismanagement or
anticipates good management. As Augustus Loring, a Boston Trustee, said in the first edition of *A
Trustee's Handbook:*

> In the hands of a good trustee, the
> Massachusetts rule is undoubtedly superior,
> since it gives him a larger opportunity to use
> his skill and ability as a financier for the

advantage of his beneficiaries; but undoubtedly
the English rule, or the New York rule, is better
adapted to inexperienced or ignorant trustees,
as much less is left to their discretion, and
unfortunately trustees are too often
appointed for consideration of friendship, and
not from consideration of their discretion or
business ability.[34]

Favorable law regarding trust investing was a significant and enduring factor allowing the Boston Trustee
to flourish in Massachusetts. Without it, the growth
of the practice would have been severely hampered.
The economic boom of international trade and shipping, followed by the textile and railroad successes,
provided Massachusetts trustees with both extraordinary assets to invest and extraordinary investment
options and latitude. Had trustees not been able to
participate in those investments, it would have great-
ly hindered the ability of the Boston Associates to
control their inheritances and would not have given
Boston Trustees a head start on what would soon arrive on the scene as their corporate competitors.

The Trustee

*And in case the said Jonathan and Francis or either of them
should not survive me, or should decline accepting said
trusts, or after having accepted the same, should .... resign
the same, or should die before having fully performed and
executed the same, then my will is that such Judge of Probate forthwith appoint one or more Trustee or Trustees in
place of such Trustee or Trustees so failing....*[1]

H AVING DISCUSSED the trust document, the
law governing trusts, and the trust property, it is time to turn our attention to the
trustee, specifically to individual professional trustees and their rise and success in Boston and their
relative absence in the rest of the United States.

The skills needed to be a good trustee are diverse
and wide-ranging, which is why finding a good trustee with all of the required attributes and capabilities
can be so difficult. First, the trustee is the owner of
the property so the investment and safeguarding of

that property is an essential function of the trustee. Often trusts will have special assets that require expertise to manage such as real estate or business interests. Even where "ordinary" assets are in the trust, the trustee must invest the assets to achieve good returns both for the beneficiaries who rely on the trust income and the remainder beneficiaries who are to receive the remainder of the trust. While the investment of the property receives much of today's attention, keeping the property safe and secure is an essential function and is among the reasons why competent and reputable trustees are required. Second, the trustee must keep track of income and principal separately, which requires knowledge of the income and principal accounting rules under the probate law that governs the trust. Third, the trustee must understand the trust document and the laws governing trusts. Fourth, the trustee must know the trust income, gift, estate, and generation-skipping tax rules for United States, the state of the trust and the states of the beneficiaries. Fifth, the trustee must often decide when and when not to distribute trust property to beneficiaries. This can be a very difficult decision for a trustee, requiring considerable judgement, foresight and communication skills. Sixth, the trustee must make all decisions in the best interests of the beneficiaries, both the current beneficiaries and future beneficiaries. And finally, the trustee must interact with the beneficiaries personably and professionally.

The profession of trusteeship is different than most other professions. Trustees often are not chosen by the people who interact with the trustee (the beneficiaries). They are, instead, first chosen by the donor and once chosen, traditionally have been very difficult to change without the trustee's own permission. Trust documents often contain the method for choosing the successor trustee; either by actually naming the successor, or by setting forth the procedure for selection. A typical provision for trustee succession for a trust with two trustees would allow the remaining trustee to fill a vacancy, sometimes with the consent of a majority of the beneficiaries. In McLean's will, the successor trustee was to be chosen by the Judge of Probate. In the trust for Ann, we see both of the original trustees ceasing to serve and successor trustees appointed.

Beneficiaries can feel trapped with a trustee who they do not like. This creates a difficult balance, as sometimes the trustee must correctly say "no" to a beneficiary. For example, how does one respond when a beneficiary whose car is in the shop asks to be reimbursed for a five day rental of a Maserati loaner? A beneficiary whose request is denied often wishes to change trustees to someone more compliant. In other circumstances, the trustee may indeed be deficient and the beneficiaries should have a right of removal. The modern trend in documents is to allow removal of trustees.[2] In addition, while state law used to make it difficult to remove trustees, the trend there, too, is to allow a court to remove the trustee unless the identity of that particular trustee is so important to the trust's success that it is a "material purpose" of the trust.[3]

Although all individual trustees must retire or die, institutions with their perpetual nature can remain trustees for the entire duration of the trust, even a "perpetuities trust" that lasts for one hundred years. Although banks and trust departments might be thought to change when they are acquired and therefore require beneficiary approval for a switch in trustees, all fifty states have laws deeming the purchase by a bank or trust department not to be a change of trustees or to require beneficiary consent.[4] Thus, many beneficiaries whose trusts began with small trust departments as their initial trustee have, over the years, seen their trustee migrate into large national trust departments containing the trusts of hundreds of other former banks.

Trustees are fiduciaries and are held to a standard higher than that of individuals acting solely in their own self-interest. They hold the trust property as owners, but for the benefit of others. As part of this higher standard, trustees are subject to several duties, the most important of which is the duty of loyalty. As revered Judge Benjamin Cardozo put it:

> A trustee is held to something stricter than the morals of the market place. Not honesty alone, but the punctilio of an honor the most sensitive, is then the standard of behavior. As to this there has developed a tradition that is unbending and inveterate. Uncompromising rigidity has been the attitude of courts of equity when petitioned to undermine the rule of undivided loyalty .... Only thus has the level of conduct for fiduciarics bccn kcpt at a level higher than that trodden by the crowd. It will not consciously be lowered by any judgment of this court.[5]

Given the difficulty and skills necessary to execute the position, it is not surprising that professional trustees were seen as necessary by Boston society and that trusteeship would begin to coalesce in a few individuals with the required skills and reputation.

Massachusetts Lawyer Trustees

It was natural that for many years the profession of trusteeship as conducted by attorneys became a side issue to their practice of law.[1]

AS WE HAVE SEEN, the origins of the Boston Trustee can be traced in part to lawyers acting as trustees for their clients and extending their role and responsibilities from what we today would call the "trusted advisor" to that of trustee:

All of these men were attorneys for, in the early days, trust business was largely a sideline for members of the bar. It was a business that could hardly be cultivated. It had to grow of its own accord. Consequently there were few if any attorney-trustees exclusively prior to 1860.[2]

Lawyers continue to act as trustees to this day, and nowhere more so than in Massachusetts. In other states, however, this dual role is often thought by lawyers to pose ethical concerns that either cannot be overcome or that lawyers do not have experience to negotiate. In addition, some lawyers worry that they may jeopardize receiving business from banks and trust offices if they or their partners are seen as competing for trust business. While these concerns may be valid, the history of lawyers serving as trustees in Massachusetts suggests that these fears are often overstated.

First, the ability to read, understand and interpret trust instruments and trust law makes lawyers, especially estate planning lawyers, the obvious choice for potential trustees. Knowledge of the law of trusts and estates and the complex gift, estate and generation-skipping tax rules is essential for a trustee. In addition, familiarity with specific state laws regarding investment and trust administration is required for anyone serving in this capacity.

Lawyers in general often enjoy poor reputations. As early as 1805, John Leland is said to have described "the swarm of lawyers who infest our land like swarms of locusts in Egypt and eat up every green thing."[3] Despite, and perhaps in contradiction to this, lawyers also often are seen as logical, thoughtful, intelligent thinkers and respected professionals. This knowledge, combined with the familiarity and trusted position of the estate planning lawyer, makes it understandable why families often look to their lawyers as trustees.

Second, some attorneys may not want to assume the role of trustee because they do not feel confident with the investment duties of trusteeship. Prior to the promulgation of the Restatement of Trusts (Third) in 1992, it was generally held that a "trustee cannot properly delegate to another the power to select investments."[4] This inhibited many non-investment professionals from serving as trustees. Larger Boston law firms solved this obstacle by hiring investment professionals to help advise them while retaining the final say on investments. However, given the post-1992 ability to delegate trust functions, it is now possible for lawyers to perform only those functions for which they are best suited and delegate the rest to other professionals without breaching any fiduciary duties.

Third, while there are sometimes ethical issues for a lawyer seeking to act as a client's trustee, those ethical issues can be dealt with properly in most situations.[5] The ethical issues begin with drafting the trust document. If a lawyer herself drafts the document in which she is named as trustee, the question arises as to whether the donor of the trust was given all of the information that was needed to make the best possible selection of trustee. If the drafting attorney suggests that she be named trustee while representing the donor, there is a conflict of interest because the lawyer has an economic interest in being named a trustee that may affect her ability to give independent advice to the client as to all of his choices and the relative merits of each potential trustee. In almost all states, these concerns can be overcome by ensuring that the drafting attorney fully discloses the potential conflicts and provides the client with adequate information regarding the factors necessary to make an informed choice of trustee.[6] Some states have passed special requirements or imposed limitations on the drafter acting as a fiduciary.[7]

Fourth, if a lawyer drafts a trust of which she will be the trustee, there is the concern that the lawyer may draft provisions into the trust that would unreasonably protect a trustee when either the donor or beneficiaries might wish to hold the trustee liable. The drafting trustee might give herself trustee powers otherwise not usually granted a trustee. Once again, restraint by the drafter not to overreach, providing full disclosure, and ensuring that the donor has the ability to consult outside counsel can result in a fair document. Of particular concern is the situation where the drafting trustee might include a provision lessening the trustee's liability standard of care. The Massachusetts Uniform Trust Code allows the drafting of such an exculpation clause by the lawyer trustee, but requires that its existence and contents are adequately communicated to the client and shifts the burden of proof should a question arise.[8]

We had hypothesized that perhaps Massachusetts state ethical rules were more accommodating to lawyers acting as fiduciaries than those of other states, but we have found no indication that Massachusetts was especially lenient in that regard. The earliest Canons of Ethics raised the issues of conflicts of interest equally throughout the country and in general have been and continue to be supportive of the idea of lawyer trustees so long as the attorney acts in the best interests of the client.[9] It may be true that lawyers outside of Massachusetts are more ready to believe that the ethical issues cannot be overcome, but the ethical rules themselves do not appear to materially differ from state to state except in rare instances.[10]

Another impediment to the lawyer acting as

trustee is the matter of legal liability insurance. Insurance companies may not be comfortable with lawyers acting as fiduciaries, believing that those responsibilities carry additional risk of liability and therefore either will not cover that activity or will narrowly define the fiduciary activities that are covered by a lawyer's liability policy. We have been told informally that lawyers with a trusteeship practice are generally charged higher premiums or are charged supplemental premiums for their legal liability insurance. In addition, lawyers may fear that, if an action is brought against them, their legal liability insurance company may attempt to limit coverage, an action that would effectively bar some lawyers from undertaking trusteeships. However, as evidenced by the multitude of attorneys serving as trustees in Massachusetts, these fears do not seem to have much real effect on Massachusetts lawyers.

Finally, a lawyer may be uninterested in acting as trustee when her other compensation might be limited. For example, a lawyer might refuse a small trusteeship if it would prevent her from representing a large and profitable estate. As we discussed earlier, Massachusetts courts have long permitted trustee compensation. In addition, the Massachusetts courts have held that the lawyer trustee may be paid as a trustee in addition to being paid as a lawyer: "We are not prepared to hold that a lawyer, acting as trustee, and having occasion to perform professional services in behalf of his trust, may not be allowed in any case to receive from the trust fund the usual professional compensation for such special services."[11]

As with all situations that pose potential conflicts of interest, a lawyer acting as trustee can either be an advantage or a disadvantage for the donor and beneficiaries. Over the course of almost two hundred years, Boston Trustees who also have been attorneys by and large have demonstrated that the duties of attorney and trustee can be performed professionally by one and the same person.

Competitive Landscape

Historically, to a greater degree than in any other area the management of private funds in a trust capacity in New England has been the province of the private trustee as opposed to trust institutions.[1]

T HE SOCIAL, ECONOMIC AND legal develop-
ments in Massachusetts were important
factors in the growth of the Boston Trustee
in the early 1800s. Also essential was the lack of legitimate competitors and the use of different types
of trustees for different types of trusts. While Massachusetts had a financially solid and important
corporation with trust powers as early as 1823 (the
Massachusetts Hospital Life Insurance Company),
in practice that company operated as an adjunct
to individual trusteeship of dynastic trusts, not as
a replacement for it. Because McLean died in 1823
and wrote his will and codicil before then, he did
not have access to a corporate trustee. As we will

see, in other states corporate trusteeship took hold as the preferred alternative for all types of trusteeship, both custodial and dynastic.

MASSACHUSETTS. We have discussed the Massachusetts Hospital Life Insurance Company as a source of capital fueling the growth of the textile industry in Massachusetts, but it also served as the first corporate trustee available to the Boston Associates. Although the ability of corporations to act as trustees was recognized as early as 1816 by the Massachusetts Supreme Judicial Court, corporations still needed a specific grant from the Legislature to act as trustee.[2] For many years no company was chartered as a trust company. The Massachusetts Hospital Life Insurance Company was the first corporation to receive this type of legislative grant.

On August 18, 1823, the Company opened for business, publishing a book of "Proposals" that set forth the types of services offered and the rules and regulations that governed its contracts. These "Proposals" set forth, in essence, annuity tables for trusts:

> The company offered two forms of trusts that were especially attractive to rich and successful fathers who doubted the abilities of their sons or who feared that their financially well-endowed daughters might be plucked by unscrupulous fortune hunters. Under the terms of these trust arrangements, known as the "strict male" and "strict female" forms, a specified sum was put on deposit for the life of the beneficiary, who was paid an income but could not under any circumstances or at any time withdraw any of the principal amount.[3]

Here, the Company, acting as trustee, did not have discretion as to whether to pay income and principal to and among trust beneficiaries, but instead promised rates of interest for capital placed with it to be paid to a specified beneficiary. Many of the founders of the Company, including Nathaniel Bowditch himself, were trustees. Although some claim the Company was the first trust company in the United States, most recognize other institutions for that distinction.[4] Whatever the case, the Company was the only "competitor" to individual trustees in the first half of the 1800s in Boston.

In a law review article entitled "The Dynastic Trust," Lawrence Friedman outlined a theoretical bifurcation of trust types. Friedman identified one type of trust as the "caretaker trust," a relatively short term trust for the benefit of those who might need special care: minor children, incompetents, and the elderly, for example. The second type of trust he called the "dynastic trust," which he identified as a truly long term trust under which the trustees had discretion to pay income and principal with the donor's purpose being "to prevent the break-up of the settlor's fortune."[5] Friedman used this paradigm to try to make some sense of historical trust law.

For our purposes, the two types of trusteeship may help to explain the ability of the Massachusetts Hospital Life Insurance Company to coexist peacefully with Boston Trustees. It appears that Boston society used the two types of trustees for different purposes. They were content to have the Company care for "caretaker trusts" for specific individuals where annuity-like returns were appropriate, but preferred to have Boston Trustees care for "dynastic trusts" for multiple generations of their families where their financial legacy was to be managed and controlled into the future.

In contrast to the *Harvard College v. Amory* standard, as the "Proposals" put it, the directors of the Company had "always viewed the safety of the Capital, rather the greatness of the income,"[6] as the fundamental standard for investing the Company's trusts. The funds placed with the Company tended to be smaller and held adjunct to other irrevocable trusts. Although the Proposals claimed advantages of using the Company rather than private trustees, the Massachusetts Hospital Life Insurance Company was not a true competitor to private individual trustees and instead perhaps even offered a complementary service.

This view is bolstered by understanding that it was an institution that was controlled by the Boston Associates. During the first century of the existence of the Massachusetts Hospital Life Insurance Company, a full third of its officers and directors were drawn from only eighteen of Boston's wealthiest and most socially prominent families.[7] A breakdown of the names of the holders of trust accounts at the Company in 1830 makes clear that the mercantile family groups who created the Company were using it as an instrument to serve at least some of their trust needs. Of interest in Bowditch's table in the Company history is the fact that 45 of the 783 trusts listed "executor" and "trustees" as the depositor.[8] Executors and trustees could use the Company for annuity-like returns for trusts and estates where no trustee discretion was required.

For us, it is also noteworthy that the history of the Company states that Ann McLean was the beneficiary of two "G" trusts that were established totaling $40,259 by her trustees, Jonathan and Francis Amory.[9] Of the five deposit types of contracts, the "G" form was the most popular trust contract. It was for a five-year renewable term with the principal repaid in full at the end.[10] It is not known whether these were the funds received by Ann outright under John McLean's will or from her inheritance from her family. In either event, it is possible that these deposits were used to diversify her investments to reduce her personal reliance on the returns from the manufacturing stocks at issue in the *Harvard College v. Amory* case.

10 MILE MARKER MILTON, MASSACHUSETTS
In 1823, the year of his death, John McLean placed mile markers six through ten out from Boston to his birthplace, Milton, Massachusetts. His business partner, Isaac Davenport, completed the work after McLean's death and had McLean's name inscribed on the stones.

While the Massachusetts Hospital Life grew rapidly at the outset, its growth slowed after 1830:

> The rapid growth in deposits through 1830 and the slowing down thereafter raises the interesting question why the earlier pace of growth was not maintained. No clear answer can be given, nor is there any evidence that the officers of the company ever gave the matter consideration. It may be that the pace slackened because the company had met most of the existing needs for service. The mercantile families, too, may have been investing more of their capital directly in new business opportunities. The heavy investments in the textile industry and railroads after 1830 could well have left less money available for the Massachusetts Hospital Life than in such years of depression as 1828 and 1829. Or it may also be that in the Boston community a sort of competition was growing (between person and institution for the management of funds) in which the Massachusetts Hospital Life was passive and not always the victor.[11]

We do know that, after the economic panic of 1837, the Board of Control recommended that the Company accept no new deposits "except so far as may be found necessary to enable it to fulfill the benevolent purposes for which it was incorporated."[12]

Bowditch himself seems not to have sought trust business for the Company just to obtain more assets under management, referring to the Company as a type of savings bank rather than a trust office:

A gentleman called to deposit a small sum of money in behalf of a young lady, his ward, to remain till she was of age. It was readily received. Before he retired, another gentleman entered, who happened to be a very particular friend of the actuary. He said, "Will you receive twenty or thirty thousand dollars in trust for me?" — "No, I cannot receive it from you."— "Why not from me, as well as any one else?"— "Because you can take care of the money yourself. Whenever, as at present is the case, there is so much money in possession of the company, uninvested, that it will not be a decided advantage for them to take any more, I receive it only from such as cannot take care of it themselves. For such cases especially was the company designed. It is a sort of Savings' Bank, except that it is on a larger scale than usual."[13]

The survival and viability of the Boston Trustee to this day was of course not as inevitable as it might appear from a history in which one knows the end-game. Strong corporate banks and trust companies did eventually arise to compete with individual trustees. New England Trust Company was founded in 1869; Boston Safe Deposit & Trust Company was founded in 1875; Old Colony Trust Company was chartered in 1890; and State Street Safe Deposit & Trust Company was chartered in 1891.

Some individual trustees such as Robert H. Gardiner concluded that the need for perpetual trustees with full capabilities for investing necessitated the use of a corporate trustee form. Gardiner founded Fiduciary Trust in 1928, seeking to capture the best of both alternatives. While Gardiner moved his practice to the corporate form, he retained the habit of Boston Trustees of having their sons enter the family business. Gardiner's son, Robert H. Gardiner, Jr., became the President of Fiduciary Trust in 1957.

While the allowance of trustee delegation has removed some of the advantages of the corporate trustee, the assurance of continuous existence and the mitigation of possible human error and lack of personal human frailty favored the corporate format. In 1949, *Nation's Business* published an article entitled "The Prudent Man's Last Stand."[14] The article ran on the premise that "After generations of guarding rich men's fortunes, the venerated Boston trustee is fast becoming extinct."[15] "They are wise, solemn gentlemen, as reticent and self-contained as a Boston cod."[16] After reciting the rise of the Boston Trustee, the article claimed a decline of the practice:

> But now the private Boston trustee is on his way out. Despite the skill and discretion with which he managed estates, he is finding it rough going in the complex financial world of today. He is yielding to the banks with their trust departments and expert economists, the huge investment trusts with their trained staffs. The sons of trustees, who might once have followed their fathers' footsteps, are now joining the institutions. And so are the fathers.[17]

The article went on to focus on Holbrook himself: "Holbrook . . . frankly admits there is little future in being a private trustee. 'We're making our last stand,' he says. 'Eventually the corporate trusts will take us over. After all, banks don't die.'"[18]

Holbrook's prediction was off the mark. The corporate trustees have continued to grow and consolidate, but private trustees have also thrived. While the practice of individual professional trustees in Boston may not have expanded to other parts of the country from the time of the article, it appears that the obituary for the practice in Boston was premature.

OTHER STATES. Other states do not have a robust individual professional trustee history or much of a current practice. According to Friedman, the bifurcation of trustee types based upon whether the trust was caretaker or dynastic was unique to Massachusetts. "Outside of Boston, the trust company played the role of the Boston trustee – it provided a rational institutional base for legal and business experience in drafting, forming, managing and perpetuating long-term trusts."[19] Certainly some individuals act as professional trustees outside of Massachusetts, but we have been unable to uncover documentation of that tradition in either Philadelphia or New York, the two jurisdictions we thought most likely to have produced such a practice. We *can* see that a vibrant *corporate* trustee practice arose in other jurisdictions which, when combined with the historically restrictive investment environment for trustees in those jurisdictions, may help to explain the lack of a class of individual private trustees.

In New York, The Farmers' Fire Insurance & Loan Company was incorporated in 1822 and is thought to be the first corporation to be granted trust powers on April 16, 1822.[20] Not bound by the Boston Trustees' reticence to advertise, the company advertised in the New York Evening Post on August 6, 1822. The advertisement sets forth the essential arguments for corporate trusteeship that have continued to this day: (1) perpetual existence and the avoidance of the need for court involvement in trustee succession, (2) accounts separate from the Company's general account, and (3) investing excellence.

> The Company also has power to receive, take, possess, and stand seized of any and all property that may be conveyed to them in TRUST, and to execute any and all such trust or trusts in their corporate capacity and name, in the same manner and to the same extent as any other trustee or trustees might or could lawfully do. The TRUST property will be kept, as the Charter prescribes, wholly separate from all other concerns of the Company, and cannot, in any event, be made liable for its losses or engagements. Any property so committed to them in TRUST will be invested in such manner as the party may chuse (*sic*) to direct.

> The public will readily perceive that the advantages of this Company to protect property for the benefit of orphans or others, or to answer any special purposes, either of public or private nature, are far greater than those of any individual executors or other trustees, who are always liable to casualties which no foresight can guard against: — as the numerous and frequent applications to the Court of Chancery for filling up of vacancies occasioned by death, insolvencies, and other causes, most incontestably show; — and the expense of such proceedings often swallows up

a great part of the TRUST estate. By placing
such property in the charge of this Company
which have continued succession, there can be
no danger whatever of any such casualties; as
all such property will be invested either at
discretion, in the most beneficial manner, for
the sole advantage of the party conveying the
same, or invested as the party may direct, with
in the strict provisions of any such trust.[21]

The incorporation of the New York Life Insurance &
Trust Company in 1830 created a fast growing corporate trust company which held deposits in trust of
over $2.5 million by 1833 and $3.5 million by 1840.[22]

Other states also had early corporate trust competitors. The Morris Canal and Banking Company
of New Jersey was granted trust powers in 1824.[23]
The Pennsylvania Company for Insurance of Lives
and Granting Annuities received trust powers February 26, 1836.[24] The Connecticut Life & Trust Company was incorporated with trust powers in 1833.

As was true with the Massachusetts Hospital Life
Company, many of these trust deposits were more
like annuities than discretionary trusts, but we have
found no definitive record of relative amounts held
in each form.[25]

If individual professional trustees were ever a factor in states other than Massachusetts, they are not
a significant factor today. Did the profession take
hold and die out, or did corporate competition and
inadequate legal and social support prevent the
practice from taking hold? In most cases, we can
infer that the lack of legal and cultural support together with strong corporate competition explains
the lack of individual professionals in other states.

James G. Smith's *The Development of Trust Companies in the United States* does have one table which we reproduce here that appears to show a switch from individual to corporate trusteeship through the ownership of railroad mortgages as investments. Smith hypothesized that the term of bond issues increasing from 50 to 100 years made donors realize the need for an "immortal trustee" causing them to prefer corporate trustees over individuals.[26] Whatever the reason, the move from individual trustees to corporate trustees as owners of railroad mortgages from 1850 on is striking.

PERCENTAGES OF RAILROAD MORTGAGES OWNED
BY INDIVIDUAL AND CORPORATE TRUSTEES

	Individual		Corporate		Total
	No.	%	No.	%	No.
1830–39	3	100%		0%	3
1840–49	18	100%		0%	18
1850–59	158	97%	5	3%	163
1860–69	146	90%	17	10%	163
1870–79	227	64%	128	36%	355
1880–89	183	23%	616	77%	799
1890–99	30	5%	634	95%	664[27]

The inception of great trusts in Massachusetts prior to the establishment of a true competitive corporate trustee was an important factor in the head start and strong foothold of the Boston Trustee, an advantage that has never been fully relinquished.

Individual and Corporate
Trustees: A Comparison

*The greater advantages offered by the trust company are
so palpable, are becoming from day to day more clearly
defined in the public mind, that the individual must give
way to the corporate fiduciary.*[1]

S INCE THE EARLIEST days of professional trusteeship, corporate trustees have attempted to
contrast the benefits they offer with those of
the individual trustee. The prevalence of the Boston
Trustee was noted in a brochure published in 1904
by the Old Colony Trust Company:

> In no other State is the formation of trusts
> under wills and other instruments looked upon
> with more favor than in Massachusetts, and
> yet it is almost the only State where the old

custom of appointing individuals to execute
these trusts has not been largely superseded
by the appointment of Trust Companies.[2]

Even the Massachusetts Hospital Life Insurance
Company in its Proposals, despite its unique relationship with and control by men who were themselves private trustees, stated that "the business will
be transacted by the Company at much less expense
than is usual in private trusts, without any of the
difficulties arising from the resignation or death
of trustees, or the losses which might ensure from
bankruptcy."[3]

As late as 1908, *Trust Companies Magazine* published a "Special Correspondence" from Boston
that attacked the continued success and recognized
reputation of the private trustee. The article sounds
more like a call to arms than a mere reporting of the
facts:

> In Boston there is a distinct class of lawyers
> who confine their attention to trusteeships.
> Their influence is powerful and their
> popularity undimmed by the growth of trust
> companies in the city. They are men of great
> shrewdness who have mastered the many
> complex laws governing the execution of trusts,
> investments of trust funds and are credited
> with abundant learning as to all the
> technicalities of the profession. They control
> many of the largest estates and trusteeships
> of the State.[4]

The author was so clearly perplexed as to why the
Boston Trustees persevered; he then backhandedly

accused the private trustees of failing to pay tax on their trusts: "There is no intention of placing all professional trustees in the category of tax-dodgers, but the fact remains that the opportunities for immunity in this respect are greater than exercised by the corporate trustee."[5]

The writer concluded that lack of publicity was the only possible explanation for the discrepancy between Boston and other areas of the country: "All the arguments are on the side of the trust company. Publicity is the thing which will solve this drawback."[6]

A Trustee's essential duties are the duties: (1) of loyalty, (2) to exercise reasonable care and skill, (3) to give, keep, and render accounts and provide information, (4) to take and control trust property, (5) to enforce claims and defend the trust, (6) of impartiality, and (7) to make trust property productive. In modern trusteeship, the individual professional trustee, especially when part of a trustee office, is able to fulfill those duties as well as a corporate trustee.

Traditionally, the beneficiary was thought to have a right to expect that the trustee would personally perform all of the duties of the trust that he could reasonably be required to perform.[7] At a minimum, a trustee could not delegate the entire administration of the trust to another person or institution. While this prohibition against delegation may have been overemphasized in the past,[8] over the years it has been transformed into a tacit recommendation to delegate when it would be helpful. In fact, in some states, the trustee is in fact now under a possible *duty* to delegate if the trust would benefit from the delegation.[9] Under modern trust law, trustees who delegate properly are given a safe harbor from liability for the actions of the delegee in certain circumstances.[10] Many individual professional trustees have high levels of expertise in investment and fund management within their offices. However, individual trustees have the right to delegate those duties if they feel their skills are not sufficient. Therefore, the individual professional trustee can be in an equal position, from the viewpoint of skill and access to advice and information, as the corporate trustee.

Many of the apparent advantages of a larger institution are achieved by the common practice of Boston Trustees to join together in partnerships or corporations to create offices of trustees. Individual trustees without the support of an office are at a disadvantage to the trust offices of larger banks or corporate offices. It would be unusual for all of the expertise needed to act as a responsible modern trustee to reside in one person. Offices of individual professional trustees allow for specialists in administration, investing and the law to provide aid and advice without requiring the trustee to increase his fees.

"Deep pockets" is often cited as a reason for preferring the large corporate trustee to the individual. If a litigable error is made and the beneficiaries have to sue the trustee, a bank is more likely to have sufficient assets to satisfy a costly judgment than an individual trustee or his office. Many institutional corporate trustees have assets far in excess of most individuals and, if execution on a judgment is required, there is a valid argument in favor of the corporate trustee. This can be somewhat mitigated by an office of individual trustees where greater capital may back the trustee. Insurance policies may be purchased by the individual trustee to compensate wronged beneficiaries up to the policy limit. That said, in general, the large national institution is in a better position to pay large claims for breaches of fiduciary duty. But while the bank may have greater capital, because an individual professional trustee is often personally liable, he may be more vigilant and attentive to the beneficiaries and the trust than a corporate trust officer where any loss will be absorbed by the corporation.

Another apparent advantage of the corporate trustee is its perpetual nature. The institutional trustee never dies, while death is certain for the individual trustee, inevitably requiring the naming of a successor. Here again, offices of Boston Trustees with succession-ready younger members can reduce this risk. Holbrook argued that the apparent corporate trustee advantage of permanence and lack of a lifespan was a misperception:

> Much has been said of the desirability of permanence and continuity in the management of trust funds. There is no doubt that the hazards of human life emphasize the frailty of an individual before the assaults of time. Confidence in a person, however, is still a major requirement, by both the owner of wealth and the beneficiary of his bounty. The stone and mortar of an institution may not change, but its personnel are still subject to the laws of life and death.[11]

In addition, corporate trustees have merged and been bought and sold to an extraordinary extent over the past few decades. This "change" of trustee arising from a merger is by statute, case law, or regulatory authority, not a change of trustee that the beneficiaries must approve, but is a change nonetheless.[12] The donor may choose a specific corporate trustee, but has no recourse if their choice of trust company changes hands. In the words of Boston Trustee, E. Sohier Welch:

> Is it not better for a family to be given recurrent opportunity to approve or disapprove the management of its affairs, by the selection of a succeeding trustee, than to be permanently in the hands of a corporation whose whole character may have changed with a change in the officers and directors, or through a merger or a sale?[13]

Some donors and beneficiaries may be comforted by the fact that bank trust departments are more regulated than both the individual trustee and large trust offices. Trust departments of national banks are regulated by the Office of the Comptroller of the Currency. State bank trust departments of banks that are members of the Federal Reserve are regulated by the Federal Reserve and by state bank regulators. While the regulation by the Securities and Exchange Commission (S.E.C.) or the state securities commission of individual trustees or trust offices is extensive and increasing, that of a bank trustee remains more pervasive and regular. In 1942, the S.E.C. agreed with Boston Trustee Augustus P. Loring, Jr., that it should not regulate him as an investment adviser to *others*. Loring argued that as trustee, he owned the trust property and therefore was managing the trust investments for *himself* as trustee.[14] For many years, Boston Trustees relied upon this exemption to not register as investment

advisers with the s.e.c. The increasing regulation of
all investment advisers, the rise of state regulation
and the probability that the s.e.c. would not continue to recognize this exception from investment adviser regulation for professional trustees, has caused
most professional trustees to register with the s.e.c.,
an action that has increased the safeguards for beneficiaries by adding investment regulation oversight
to many of the larger Boston Trustee offices. A specific narrow exemption from registration under the
Investment Advisers Act of 1940 continues to exist
for a "family office."¹⁵ Some of the law firm trustee
offices have not (yet) been regulated by the s.e.c. or
the states. An s.e.c. exemption for "private advisers" with fewer than fifteen clients was eliminated
by the Dodd-Frank Wall Street Reform and Consumer Protection Act in July of 2011.¹⁶ Legal ethical rules provide some safeguards for beneficiaries
of trusts trusteed by lawyer trustees, but these firms
or individual lawyers are not overseen with the same
level of regulation as the regulated trustee offices or
banks. Donors and beneficiaries who remain concerned about trustee misconduct and are not reas-
sured by the systems and regulation of individual
trustee offices will continue to prefer bank trustees
despite some of the advantages of Boston Trustees.

Personal attention, lack of corporate bureaucracy
and choice of the person who will exercise discretion
are the advantages most often cited for the choice of
the individual trustee over corporate trustees.

> Yet in one very important respect the corporate
> fiduciary may be deficient – it is a *corporation*,
> not a natural person, and the service it per-
> forms as trustee is a *personal* service in part.

Individual and Corporate Trustees: A Comparison

The trust company may give the *cestui que trust* more efficient administration than an individual trustee could, but it is claimed by some that there is lacking the personal relationship and sympathy which may at times be of great importance to the beneficiary.[17]

The proponents of individual trustees fear that the corporate fiduciary's discretionary distribution decisions will be made by a committee and will not be made as quickly or with the same personal connection to the beneficiaries as they might be by an individual trustee. Thomas Leaming perhaps put it most prosaically, "No doubt there are some objectionable features in having for a trustee a corporation, which has neither a body to be kicked nor a soul to be damned."[18] Certainly, the attention of an excellent trust officer on behalf of the corporate fiduciary and a proper culture in the trust department of thc corporation can ameliorate these possible disadvantages.

Both corporate trusteeship and professional individual trusteeship have advantages and disadvantages. The advantages of the Boston Trustee – personal relationships, flexibility, specific experience and skill – have continued to be sufficient to lead many donors and beneficiaries to choose them as key advisors to and caretakers for their families and their fortunes.

The Franklin Fund

And, as it is presumed that there will always be found in Boston virtuous and benevolent citizens, willing to bestow a part of their time in doing good to the rising generation, by superintending and managing this institution gratis, it is hoped, that no part of the money will at any time be dead, or be diverted to other purposes, but be continually augmenting by the interest.[1]

PERHAPS THE MOST iconic example that is used to demonstrate the investing prowess of the Boston Trustees and to burnish their image is that of the Franklin Trusts. The *investing* expertise imputed to the Boston Trustee from the management of this fund is probably undeserved, however the prudence exhibited is worthy of respect. Nonetheless, the reputation of the Boston Trustee continues to be enhanced by the story.

Benjamin Franklin died in 1790, leaving a will and codicil which left £1,000 ($4,444.44[2]) each to the cities of Boston and Philadelphia. The money was to be lent to young married "artificers" under the age of 25 at the rate of 5% interest and was to be held for a total of 200 years, by which time Franklin estimated that the fund would be worth £4,061,000.[3] Franklin himself was aware that his plan might go awry:

> Considering the accidents to which all human affairs and projects are subject in such a length of time, I have, perhaps, too much flattered myself with a vain fancy, that these dispositions, if carried into execution, will be continued without interruption, and have the effects proposed.[4]

BENJAMIN FRANKLIN STATUE (1856)
Old City Hall, Boston, Massachusetts
Richard S. Greenough, Sculptor
Supposedly Boston's first public statue of a person

Thus, the investment expected by Franklin was in loans to individuals on good security, not in other investments. The funds loaned in Philadelphia suffered from a high proportion of defaults and suspensions of repayment which hurt investment results.[5] It soon became clear in both cities that there were insufficient possible borrowers of the funds. Therefore, the funds would need to be used for different purposes and invested in alternate ways. What resulted was a kind of financial horse race in which Boston's fund, managed by Boston Trustees, outpaced the Philadelphia fund by an extraordinary rate. We do not know the exact investments made by the two funds for their entire history or the reasons for the substantial discrepancy in their values. We do know that William Minot, a respected Boston Trustee, was the Treasurer of the Boston Fund for fifty-five years. Minot deposited $10,000 of the Fund on January 28, 1827, with the Massachusetts Hospital Life Insurance Company and made additional deposits totaling $5,950 through July 7, 1865. At the end of 1953, $125,229 still remained at the Company.[6] Upon Minot's resignation, the Mayor of Boston wrote to the Board of Aldermen:

Mr. Minot has held this important trust for the long period of fifty-five years, having accepted it in 1811. At that time it amounted to about nine thousand dollars; it has accumulated now to a sum exceeding one hundred and eleven thousand dollars, which is principally deposited with the Hospital Life Insurance Company.

The care with which this fund has been managed, and the public spirit which has

induced Mr. Minot to hold this trust for so long
a period, deserve the gratitude of our citizens.[7]

According to his account in 1866, upon Minot's re-
tirement over 99% of the Fund was invested with the
Massachusetts Hospital Life Insurance Company
with the rest invested in the Provident Institution
for Savings, the Suffolk Savings Bank and in one
loan to an individual.[8] This investment in the Massachusetts Hospital Life Insurance Company and
the banks, yielding annuity-like returns (reported by
Minot to be 5.3% annually from the Massachusetts
Hospital Life Insurance Company funds[9]) would not
have taken advantage of the discrepancy in the investing rules of the two states and the more liberal
investing rules available to Massachusetts trustees.
Whatever the cause, by 1962, with differing distributions and differing lawsuits over various aspects
of the bequests, Boston's fund was worth $1,750,000
and Philadelphia's was valued at $315,000.[10] In 1990,
those amounts were $4.5 million for Boston and $2
million for Philadelphia.[11]

E. Digby Baltzell, in his iconic book comparing the
early years of the two cities epitomizes the view of
the financial race when describing the Philadelphia
fund, "I do not know exactly how this money is being
used, but I imagine it is increasing in value just as
slowly as in the past."[12]

Fairly or unfairly, the reputation of the Boston
Trustee has been gilded by the Franklin trust tale of
the tape. Certainly prudence in investing is not to be
undervalued. "'We're not smart men,' one trustee said
recently, 'but we are prudent. If you want smart fellows, you'd better go to New York. And ask them how
they did during the crash.'"[13]

Codicil

Now you know the rest of the story.[1]

A codicil is an amendment to a will, but the word can also mean a supplement or appendix. Although not essential to our main Boston Trustee history, the tale of McLean's other bequests needs telling to avoid leaving the reader without closure to the story. Amazingly, this famous will contained a fatal flaw when it was originally written. It did not contain a residuary clause to dispose of the rest of the estate after the specific bequests. This oversight was corrected in a codicil dated one year later and one year before McLean's death, leaving everything not specifically disposed of to the Massachusetts General Hospital.

The history of the Massachusetts General Hospital recites that while Mrs. McLean received "an income probably averaging twelve per cent per annum," the Hospital received less than $20,000 of the original $25,000 at her death.[2] However, the Hospital's his-

tory also states that the residue proved to be over
$90,000.

The bequest and residue from McLean was by far
the largest amount given to the Hospital prior to
1851; it is listed in the Hospital's records as being
valued at $119,858.20.[3] As a result of the bequest
by John McLean, a Committee was appointed by
the Hospital Board of Trustees to determine how
to commemorate McLean's gift. First, Ann McLean
was given a bed at the Hospital free for life.[4] Next,
the Hospital Board commissioned Gilbert Stuart to
paint a portrait of McLean which is depicted on the
cover. Finally, the Hospital considered renaming the
Hospital in McLean's name. In the end, McLean's
name was given to the Massachusetts General Hospital insane asylum, now known as McLean Hospital. Ironically, the Asylum's administrative building
was housed in a house designed by the same Charles
Bulfinch who had designed the Franklin Crescent
house that McLean bought in 1795. Nathaniel I.
Bowditch, the Navigator's son and historian of the
Hospital, reported: "On the other hand the corporate name remained unchanged, many sons and
daughters of Massachusetts have since contributed
to it as a *State* institution, what perhaps they would
have hesitated to bestow, if it had born the name of a
private founder."[5]

After John McLean died, his wife, Ann, become
very involved in charitable work, "Suddenly, within a year of John McLean's death, the wealthy and
childless Ann burst onto the city's benevolent stage
.... Her orthodox Calvinism dictated which organi-
zations would have the benefit of her labors, and her
wealth made her an especially attractive choice for
organizational presidencies or vice-presidencies."[6]

ANN MCLEAN

As a wealthy widow, Ann sought to protect herself from the financial claims of any future husband. On August 14, 1829, Ann placed all of her own property in trust, naming John Lowell, John Amory Lowell, and her brother, Rufus G. Amory, as trustees. Ann reserved the right to appoint the property later by her will. Although she was not married, Ann provided for any later husband she might have. The trustees were to pay her what she requested. However, if they "think that my husband shall unduly influence said Ann in the expenditure of any money paid to her so that the same be not applied to her personal comfort and support or in such way as her own inclination would direct, the said Trustees may withhold said income in whole or in part."[7] The trustees were given discretion to provide for her care and were only to be liable for their "wilful default." The trust provided for annual trustee fees of 2.5% of the income, profits, and dividends from the trust property.

About one year later, on November 4, 1830, Ann married William Lee at her house at 44 Beacon Street. Lee was a diplomat, having served as Consul for the United States in Bordeaux and as Second Auditor in the War Department in Washington. John Quincy Adams attended the wedding, as did most of the Amorys.[8] Ann died September 11, 1834, of a "bilious intermitting fever"[9] and left $25,000 to Harvard College, $25,000 to the McLean Hospital, and provided for her husband the "house, horses, carriages, plate, furniture"[10] and, what was later described as, "a handsome income to be enjoyed during life."[11] Despite her generous provisions for him, Mr. Lee set loose the following unflattering portrait of Ann to his children after her death:

> I think myself it is a most extraordinary will. It shows how much influence these religious sects and these priests have over the minds of their associates. My wife was deluded by them. They courted and flattered her by placing [her] at the head of their institutions and robbed her and her family.

> She was enthusiastic, sincere, and immovable in her religious opinions, and believed in all the doctrines of that murderer Calvin. I have scolded her, read to her, coaxed her, persuaded her, but it was all in vain. You might as well attempt to throw a ray of light into a block of granite as into her mind .... She is as a spoiled [child], accustomed to govern with despotic sway all about her, and as since one must yield,

I took upon myself to yield in everything and she was happy, but I was not; on the contrary as miserable as a man could be; for in addition to her religious frenzy she was the most penurious being on earth: eternally hoarding for what she thought the cause of God. Next to Him she loved me most ardently, and seeing it I bent to all her wishes, to the astonishment of all her family and friends. Had I not done it would have both been very miserable. Had she married a rude headstrong man, she would have been a most wretched being.[12]

Ann was buried next to John McLean, his parents, Hugh and Agnes McLean, and her brother/trustee, Francis, in a tomb at the Milton Cemetery. The tomb was deconstructed by the cemetery for safety reasons and the graves are now marked by the lintel which reads "F. Amory, A.D. 1842" and the original tombstone:

THE TOMB OF JOHN MCLEAN
HUGH MCLEAN, *died December, 1799,*
aged 75 years.
AGNES MCLEAN, *died March, 1821,*
aged 82 years.
JOHN MCLEAN, *died Oct. 16, 1823,*
aged 62 years.
SARAH AMORY, *wife of Francis Amory,*
died Oct. 8, 1828, aged 49 years.
ANN LEE, *widow of John McLean and wife of*
William Lee, died Sept. 11, 1834,
aged 60 years.
FRANCIS AMORY, *died July 6, 1845,*
aged 79.

Current Boston Trustees

In the shadow of the giant investment firms that call Boston home, there is a breed of quiet, bookish money handlers who have overseen old wealth in this region for decades.[1]

BOSTON TRUSTEES as we have defined them still thrive. Of those currently practicing in this capacity, we can further divide them into more delineated groups.

There are the single family offices that offer a range of services primarily or exclusively to one family (although some are now offering services to non-family members): J. M. Forbes & Co., Howland Capital, and Saltonstall & Co. are examples of these, but there are many others.

There are firms that are in fact corporations and are somewhat closer to bank trust departments, but maintain their Boston Trustee roots: Fiduciary Trust

Company is, in our personal view, a good example of this type of firm.

Law firms with trust departments in Boston manage large sums as traditional Boston Trustees: Ropes & Gray LLP, Hemenway & Barnes LLP, Choate Hall & Stewart LLP, Goulston & Storrs PC, Nutter, McClennen & Fish LLP, Bowditch & Dewey LLP, Day Pitney LLP, Rackemann, Sawyer & Brewster and Nixon Peabody International LLP are examples of these, but there are others that provide fine services. In recent years, some of these law firms have created registered investment advisory arms to comply with S.E.C. regulations.

There are the multi-family traditional Boston Trustee offices (although at least one is partially owned by a public company). Examples include: Welch & Forbes LLC, Loring Wolcott & Coolidge Office, Rice Heard & Bigelow Inc. and Nichols & Pratt LLP. Of these, Nichols & Pratt is notable as it was founded relatively recently in 1977 when James R. Nichols and Harold I. Pratt combined their trust businesses. This firm is also the only one that we know of that remains a partnership (in the tradition of Boston Trustee offices).

Four Boston Trustee firms that we know of can trace their origins back to the inception of the profession: Rice Heard & Bigelow, Inc. (George Richards Minot and William Minot), Loring Wolcott & Coolidge Office (Nathaniel Bowditch and Nathaniel Ingersoll Bowditch), Welch & Forbes LLC (Charles A. Welch and Edward Dexter Sohier) and Fiduciary Trust Company (Robert H. Gardiner). According to Charles P. Curtis, in his 1959 article, the law firm trust department of Choate Hall & Stewart LLP also can trace itself to a well-known trustee line of Dexters.[2]

Conclusion

*Boston is the only place in America where wealth and the
knowledge of how to use it are apt to coincide.*[1]

THE EVOLUTION of trusteeship in Boston
into the Boston Trustee model was a product of economic, social and legal circumstances that combined to allow the professional
individual trustee to thrive. This combination was
apparently lacking in other cities, since in no other
city do we have any equivalent. In Boston, both the
Boston Trustee and corporate trustee flourish, providing donors with a greater choice in trustee selection than that found elsewhere.

The story of John McLean and his will has allowed
us to explain the world of trusts with a real example
while at the same time giving context to the times
and the Boston history that was central to the *Harvard College v. Amory* case and resulting law.

Perhaps the key to the continued success of the

Boston Trustee, and unquestionably one of its hallmarks, is the view begun with the early practitioners that trusteeship included the duty to give *personal* attention to the trust beneficiaries in carrying out the donor's wishes:

> But we believe that as fiduciaries and attorneys, we have a function to perform which is something more than that of investing and administering the funds entrusted to us. Like our predecessors of one hundred years ago, we look upon each client as a personal friend, or, as my grandfather used to say 'a member of our financial family.' We are interested not only in their financial welfare, but in their moral and spiritual relations with life. No problem is too intimate, too intricate or too troublesome for our attention.[2]

Certainly, the head start given to Boston Trustees allowed them to become entrenched, trusted and experienced before corporate competition arose. Whatever the cause, the institution has in the over seventy-five years since Holbrook first published his brief thoughts, "weathered many a gale" and appears able to "adjust [itself] to the *tempo* of the times" while retaining an important place in trusteeship in this country.

The Will and Codicil of John McLean

In the name of God, Amen.

I John McLean of Boston in the county of Suffolk and Commonwealth of Massachusetts, Merchant, being of sound and disposing mind and memory do make, publish and declare, this my last will and testament, in manner and form following.

First. I give and devise to my beloved wife Ann McLean, my dwelling house situated in Beacon Street in said Boston together with the stable out-houses belonging thereto with all the land under, adjoining to and appurtenant to the same, together also with all the privileges and appurtenances, belonging to the same, to have and hold to her said Ann, her heirs and assigns forever.

ITEM. I give and bequeath to my said wife Ann McLean, all the house-hold furniture, house-hold stores, horses and carriages of which I may die possessed, together with my Pew, in the Federal Street Meeting House, to and for her own use and behoof forever.

ITEM. I give and bequeath to my said wife Ann McLean, the sum of thirty five thousand dollars, to and for her own use and behoof forever, to be paid to her by my executors, as soon as conveniently may be after my decease.

ITEM. I give and bequeath to Jonathan Amory of said Boston, Merchant, and Francis Amory of said Boston, Merchant, jointly, the sum of fifty thousand dollars in trust nevertheless to loan the same upon ample and sufficient security, or to invest the same in safe and productive stock, either in the public funds, Bank shares or other stock, according to their best judgment and discretion, hereby enjoining on them particular care and attention in the choice of funds, and in the punctual collection of the dividends, interest and profits thereof, and authorizing them sell out, re-invest & change the said loans and stocks from time to time, as the safety and interest of said trust fund, may in their judgment

[139]

require. And this bequest is upon the further trust, that said
sum of fifty thousand dollars so invested, shall constitute a
separate and distinct fund, the profits and income thereof to
be received and collected by said Trustees and paid over to
my said wife Ann McLean, in quarterly or semi-annual payments, as shall be most convenient for said Trustees, for and
during the term of her natural life. And this bequest of fifty
thousand dollars is upon the further trust, that the Trustees
will, after the decease of my said wife, pay over, transfer and
deliver one half, in actual value of the said entire fund, to the
President and Fellows of Harvard College, the income and
profits whereof shall be exclusively and forever appropriated
to the support of a Professor of Ancient and Modern History, at that College. And it shall be the duty of the Professor
established on this foundation, to deliver annually a course
of public lectures in his department, for the benefit of the
students at said College, free of expense to them, to such
classes, at such times, and under such regulations, as the
President and Fellows of said College may from time to time,
direct and appoint. If however, from any cause, the fund so
to be paid over to said President and Fellows, shall not yield
an income sufficient for the support of such Professor, they
are hereby authorized to add the income thereof to the principal for such length of time as may be necessary to increase
said fund to a sum, the income whereof may be sufficient for
the support of such Professor. But if, after the receipt of said
fund by said President and Fellows, and after the same shall
have accumulated sufficiently to yield an income adequate to
the support of such Professor, there shall be a vacancy in the
office of such Professor, for the space of two years continually, my will and direction is, and this gift to said President
and Fellows is upon the trust that they will pay over the
income of such fund which may accrue during such term of
two years, and during such vacancy, to the Trustees of the
Massachusetts General Hospital. If however, a professorship
of Ancient and Modern History shall have been established
at Harvard University, at the time when such fund is to
be paid to said President and Fellows, and they shall be at
liberty to appropriate and apply the income of said fund to
the support of such other professorship, as they may deem
fit and useful, and which may be best adapted, in their judg-

ment to promote the interests of literature and science, and advance the reputation of the University. And this bequest of fifty thousand dollars, is so made as aforesaid, upon the further trust, the said Trustees will, after the decease of my said wife, pay over, transfer and deliver the other moiety in actual value, of the fund constituted and set apart as aforesaid, to the Trustees of the Massachusetts General Hospital, to be by them held, appropriated and applied to the general charitable objects and purposes of that institution.

ITEM. I give and bequeath to the said Jonathan Amory and Francis Amory jointly, the further sum of ten thousand dollars, in trust nevertheless to be loaned or invested in the manner herein before directed, to constitute a fund, and to pay over, appropriate and apply one half of the profits and income of said fund annually, for the support, maintenance and education of John McLean Bethune, son of Mr. George Bethune, until he shall arrive at the age of twenty one years; and when said John shall have arrived at the age of twenty one years, then to pay over him the whole amount of said fund with the accumulation thereof, if they think it expedient, or, in their discretion, to pay over to him such part thereof as they shall judge proper, and retain such part thereof as they may think proper, and for such time as they may think proper, paying the income and profits thereof annually to him said John, acting in this particular in such manner, as shall in their judgment be best calculated to promote the interests of said John McLean Bethune, due regard being had to his capacity, conduct and character. And in case said John shall happen to die before arriving at the age of twenty one years, or before the said fund shall have been wholly applied and paid, then in further trust, that the income and profits thereof, and also the capital thereof, shall be held, applied and appropriated for the support, and education, use and benefit of George Bethune, brother of said John, in the same manner in all respects, as hereinbefore directed in regard to said John. And if both die in like manner, then the said sum is to remain in the same manner as if this bequest had not been made.

ITEM. I give and bequeath to such of the children of Mr.

Thomas Amory, brother of my said wife, as may be living at
the time of my decease, the sum of ten thousand dollars, to
be equally divided between them.

ITEM. I give and bequeath to Patience Holbrook Lillie of
Dorchester in the county of Norfolk, Spinster, the sum of
three thousand dollars.

ITEM. I give and bequeath to John Bois now of Dorchester
in the county of Norfolk the sum of twenty five hundred
dollars.

ITEM. I give and bequeath to the Minister and Deacons of
the Congregational Society in Milton in the county of Norfolk, and their successors in office, the sum of two thousand
dollars, in trust nevertheless to loan or invest the same so
that the principal thereof may be at once safe and productive, and the interest and income thereof to be annually,
in the three winter months, paid over and distributed for
the relief and comfort of such person or persons, belonging
to the said parish, and not paupers, as the Minister and Deacons of the said parish, for the time being, shall judge and
determine to be suitable objects for such relief. And it shall
be the duty of the Minister and Deacons of the said parish
after the receipt of said sum, to meet together once every
year, in the month of November, to determine upon and
designate the person or persons to whom and the proportions in which the said profits and income of said fund, shall
be paid over and distributed, through the three following
winter months, and the names of the persons so designated,
and the amount and proportion to be paid to them respectively, shall then be entered in a book to be kept for that
purpose. And in case such minister and deacons shall be
equally divided upon any question touching such designation and distribution, the Minister shall have a casting voice
therein. And in case of a vacancy in the office of minister,
such designation and distribution shall and may be made by
the deacons of said parish for the time being.

ITEM. I give and bequeath to the Minister and Deacons of
the Congregational Society in Federal Street in said Boston,

and their successors in office, the sum of two thousand dollars, in trust nevertheless to loan or invest the same, so that the principal thereof may be safe and productive, and the interest and income thereof to be annually, in the three winter months, paid over and distributed for the relief and comfort of such person or persons, belonging to said Society and not paupers, as the minister and deacons of the said Society for the time being shall judge and determine to be suitable objects for such relief. And it shall be the duty of the Minister and Deacons of said Society, after the receipt of said sum, to meet together once every year, in November, to determine upon and designate the person or persons to whom, and the proportions in which the said profits and income shall be distributed and paid over during the three following winter months, and the names of the persons so designated, and the amount and proportion to be paid to them respectively, shall be entered in a book, to be kept for that purpose. And in case such Minister and Deacons shall be equally divided on any question touching such designation or distribution, the Minister shall have a casting voice therein. And in case of a vacancy in the office Minister, such designation and distribution shall and may be made by the Deacons of the said Society for the time being.

ITEM. I give and bequeath to the Boston Female Asylum, the sum of five hundred dollars. And reposing full and entire confidence in the ability, fidelity and diligence of the said Jonathan Amory and Francis Amory, and not doubting that they will faithfully and conscientiously discharge and execute the trusts hereby reposed in them, and being desirous of relieving them from the burden of procuring sureties for large sums, I do request and direct that they may not be required to give any other than their own bonds respectively without sureties, conditional for the performance and execution of the said trusts; And I do order and direct that they shall not be held responsible for the acts, doings and default of each other, but shall simply be accountable respectively each for his own acts, doings and defaults, as such Trustees.

And in case the said Jonathan and Francis or either of them should not survive me, or should decline accepting said trusts, or after having accepted the same, should by writing under their hands respectively, addressed to the Judge of Probate having jurisdiction of this my will, resign the same, or should die before having fully performed and executed the same, then my will is that such Judge of Probate forthwith appoint one or more Trustee or Trustees in place of such Trustee or Trustees so failing and thereupon that the several bequests herein before made to them in trust, are hereby transferred to, and shall take effect and vest in the Trustee or Trustees so appointed, to be held by them upon the like trusts in all respects, as are herein before specified.

And I do hereby constitute and appoint the said Jonathan Amory and Francis Amory to be joint executors of this my last will and testament, hereby revoking all wills and testamentary dispositions of every nature and description by me heretofore made.

FIRST CODICIL

Be it remembered that I John McLean of Boston, Merchant, having made and executed my last will and testament bearing date August thirtieth Anno Dom. one thousand eight hundred and twenty one, do hereby in addition thereto, declare and dispose as follows, _____ viz _____.
First. In consequence of the decease of Mr. John Bois, since the execution of my said will, the bequest therein made to him, is revoked and declared null.

The Will and Codicil of John McLean

Secondly. I do give, devise and bequeath all the rest and residue of my property and estate, real, personal or mixed wherever situated, or however designated or described, which I may leave at my decease, and which is not mentioned or disposed of in my said will, to the Trustees of the Massachusetts General Hospital to be appropriated and applied according to their best judgment and discretion to all and singular, the humane, scientific and charitable objects and purposes for which that institution was established.

[Attestation and Signatures Omitted]

List of Illustrations

Cover Photograph – Gilbert Stuart, *John McLean*, 1824. Oil on canvas. Photo courtesy of McLean Hospital Archives, Belmont, Mass.

Chapter Illustrations: Edouart, Augustin-Amant-Constant-Fidèle, 1789–1861, artist.

List of Illustrations

NOTES

Preface
1. Seuss, *Oh The Places You'll Go!* (New York: Random House Books for Young Readers, 1990), 41.

Introduction
1. Sheehan, William J., "Unique to Boston are the Famous 'Boston Trustees,'" *Boston Evening Transcript*, July 28, 1934, 3.
2. Church, Eric; Church, Brandon; Beavers, Brett, *How 'Bout You.* Capital Nashville. Originally released January 30, 2006.
3. Holbrook, Donald, *The Boston Trustee* (Boston: Marshall Jones Company, 1937), vii.
4. Ibid., 37.

The Donor: John McLean
1. Will of John McLean. Judicial Archives, Massachusetts Archives, Boston, Massachusetts. See Page 139 for complete text.
2. Weeks, Lyman Horace, *A History of Paper-Manufacturing in the United States, 1690–1916* (New York: The Lockwood Trade Journal Company, 1916), 24.
3. Leonard, Eugenie Andruss, "Paper as a Critical Commodity During the American Revolution," *The Pennsylvania Magazine of History and Biography* vol. 74, No. 4 (1950), 489.
4. Cullen, James Bernard, ed., *The Story of the Irish in Boston: Together with Biographical Sketches of Representative Men and Noted Women* (Boston: James B. Cullen & Company, 1889), 188.
5. Quincy, Josiah, *The History of Harvard University*, vol. II (Cambridge: Folsom, Wells, and Thurston, 1840), 54.
6. Cullen, *The Story of the Irish*, 189.
7. Eaton, Cyrus, *Annals of the Town of Warren, in Knox County, Maine, with the Early History of St. George's, Broad Bay, and the Neighboring Settlements on the Waldo Patent*, second ed. (Hallowell: Masters & Livermore, 1877), 128.
8. *Milton Records: Births, Marriages and Deaths 1662–1843* (Boston: Alfred Mudge & Son, Printers, 1900).
9. Place, Charles A., *Charles Bulfinch, Architect and Citizen* (New York: Da Capo Press, 1968), 64.
10. Cullen, *The Story of the Irish*, 189.
11. *The Universal Masonic Library, A Republication, in Thirty Volumes, of all the Standard Publications in Masonry*, vol. IV (New York: Jno. W. Leonard & Co., 1855), 155.
12. Davis, William Thomas, *Professional and Industrial History of Suffolk County, Massachusetts*, vol. II (Boston: The Boston History Company, 1894), 246 and 256.
13. Cullen, *The Story of the Irish*, 189.

Notes

14. Committee on Claims, *French Spoliations: A Condensed Report of the Findings of the Court of Claims in Each Case Named in the Proposed Amendment by Senator Lodge to H.R. 19115* (Washington: Government Printing Office, 1912).
15. Cullen, *The Story of the Irish*, 189.
16. Ibid.
17. According to the Federal Reserve Bank of Minneapolis Consumer Price Index (estimate) 1800 - . Using a 2014 CPI of 709.9 and a 1823 CPI of 36.
18. Bowditch, Nathaniel I., *A History of the Massachusetts General Hospital*, reprint edition (New York: Arno Press & The New York Times, 1972), 64.
19. According to the Federal Reserve Bank of Minneapolis Consumer Price Index (estimate) 1800 - . Using a 2014 CPI of 709.9 and a 1823 CPI of 36.

The Trust Document

1. Lehman, Milton, "The Prudent Man's Last Stand," *Nation's Business* (March 1949), 83.
2. Mass. Gen. Laws, ch. 203E, §408 (2012).
3. In 1929, contractors Guido, Leonard, and Joseph Rugo established a fund governed by an oral agreement to support their construction business. In 1941 and 1944, the fund purchased shares in the Boston Braves Baseball team, a team owned by construction magnate Lou Perini. In 1949, the Rugo brothers sued each other as to the ownership of the fund and whether it was owned by their corporation or by a trust. *Rugo v. Rugo*, 325 Mass. 612 (1950).
4. Amory, Thomas C., *Memoir of Hon. Richard Sullivan* (Cambridge: University Press, 1885), 15.

The Boston Trustee

1. Sheehan, "Unique to Boston," 3.
2. Stebbings, Chantal, *The Private Trustee in Victorian England* (Cambridge: Cambridge University Press, 2002), 9.
3. Sheehan, "Unique to Boston," 3.
4. Lehman, "Prudent Man's Last Stand," 31.
5. Sheehan, "Unique to Boston," 3.
6. Ibid.
7. Ibid.
8. Lehman, "Prudent Man's Last Stand," 82.

Origins of the Boston Trustee

1. "City of Boston," *Fortune*, vol. VII, No. 2 (Feb. 1933), 36.
2. Holbrook, *The Boston Trustee*, 12.

3. Curtis, Charles P., "Manners and Customs of the Boston Trustee," 1958 *A.B.A. Sec. Real Prop. Prob. & Tr. Proc.* (1958), 40.

4. Dexter, Philip, *Harvard College Twenty-Fifth Anniversary Report, Class of 1889, 1889–1914* (Cambridge: Harvard University Press, 1914), 327.

5. *Bates v. Arizona*, 433 U.S. 350 (1977).

6. Sheehan, "Unique to Boston," 3.

7. Ibid.

8. *List of Persons, Copartnerships, and Corporations, Who Were Taxed Twenty-Five Dollars and Upwards in the City of Boston in the Year 1848* (Boston: J.H. Eastburn, 1849).

9. *"Our First Men:" A Calendar of Wealth, Fashion and Gentility, Containing a list of those persons taxed in the city of Boston credibly reported to be worth one hundred thousand dollars; with biographical notices of the principal persons,* revised edition (Boston: All the Booksellers, 1846), 33.

10. *"Our First Men,"* 19.

11. Foote, Henry Wilder, *In Memory of Charles Pelham Curtis* (Boston: J.H. Eastburn, 1864), 4.

12. Curtis, "Manners and Customs."

13. Brooks, Edward, *A Correspondence Between Edward Brooks and John A. Lowell, with Remarks by Edward Brooks, Referring to Documents Annexed* (Boston: S.N. Dickinson, 1847), 55.

14. Reno, Conrad, *The Judiciary and Bar of New England for the Nineteenth Century,* vol. III (Boston: The Century Memorial Publishing Co., 1901), 215.

15. *The Boston Directory; Containing Names of the Inhabitants; Their Occupations, Places of Business and Dwelling Houses; with Lists of the Streets, Lanes and Wharves, the City Officers, Public Offices, and Banks, and Other Useful Information* (Boston: John H.A. Frost and Charles Stimpson, Jr., 1823).

16. *The Boston Directory; Containing Names of the Inhabitants; Their Occupations, Places of Business and Dwelling Houses; with Lists of the Streets, Lanes and Wharves, the City Officers, Public Offices, and Banks, and Other Useful Information* (Boston: Sampson, Davenport, & Co., 1873).

17. *List of Persons Taxed 1848.*

18. *"Our First Men,"* 39.

19. "Noteworthy Union of 'Boston Trustees,'" *Boston Evening Transcript,* Jan. 5, 1935.

20. Reno, *The Judiciary,* 622.

21. Welch, Charles A., "A Sketch by Charles A. Welch, 1815–1901" [typescript]. Collection of the Massachusetts Historical Society, Boston, Massachusetts, 7.

22. Minot, William, *Private Letters of William Minot* (Privately Printed, 1895), 10-11.

23. Loring, Augustus P., Jr., *Nathaniel Bowditch (1773–1838) of*

Notes

Salem and Boston Navigator, etc. (New York: Newcomen Society, 1950), 9–10.

24. Ibid., 17.
25. Bowditch, Henry Ingersoll, *Nat the Navigator, A Life of Nathaniel Bowditch For Young Persons* (Boston: Lee and Shepard, 1870).
26. Bowditch, Nathaniel, trans., *Mécanique Céleste, with a Memoir of the Translator,* volume IV (Boston: Charles C. Little and James Brown, 1839), 41.
27. Loring, *Nathaniel Bowditch,* 18.
28. Ibid.
29. Although he ceased his education as a child, Bowditch was given an honorary degree by Harvard and was elected an Overseer and a member of the Harvard Corporation. He declined a Professorship of Mathematics at the College.
30. Hall, Peter Dobkin, and Marcus, George E., "Why Should Men Leave Great Fortunes to Their Children?," in *Inheritance and Wealth in America,* ed. Miller, Robert K., and McNamee, Stephen J. (New York: Plenham Press, 1998), 154.
31. Bowditch, *Mécanique Céleste,* 97.
32. "Jonathan Ingersoll Bowditch," *Proceedings of the American Academy of Arts and Sciences,* vol. 24, (May 1888–1889), 437.
33. "Francis C. Welch Claimed By Death," *The Boston Globe,* Feb. 28, 1919, 4.
34. Unattributed obituary of Edward Dexter Sohier, Massachusetts Historical Society Ms. S-827 "Attachment 1." Collection of the Massachusetts Historical Society, Boston, Massachusetts.
35. "News From the Classes," *Harvard Graduates Magazine,* vol. XVII, (1908–1909), 319.
36. Sheehan, "Unique to Boston," 3.
37. Curtis, "Manners and Customs," 41.
38. Fiduciary Trust Company, *A New Approach to Trust Management* (Boston: Investment Counsel Trust Company, 1940), 6–7.
39. Loring, *Nathaniel Bowditch,* 9–10.
40. Holbrook, *The Boston Trustee,* 14–15.
41. Holbrook, Donald, *An Unlikely Firemaster* (Fitzwilliam: Fire Protection Research International, 1968), 11.
42. Ibid., 16.

The Property: Economic and Social Backdrop

1. Adams, Russell B., *The Boston Money Tree* (New York: Thomas Y. Crowell Company, 1977), 221.
2. Shlakman, Vera, *Economic History of a Factory Town: A Study of Chicopee, Massachusetts.* Smith College Studies in History: v. 20, no. 1–4 (New York: Octagon Books, 1969), 31.

3. Holmes was a Brahmin himself. Born in 1809, he attended prep school at Phillips Academy in Andover, Harvard College and Harvard Medical School. Holmes married Amelia Lee Jackson, part of the textile Jackson family.

4. Holmes, Oliver Wendell, *Elsie Venner: A Romance of Destiny* (London: Routledge, Warne and Routledge, 1861), 2–4.

5. Glaeser, Edward L., "Reinventing Boston: 1640–2003," (Harvard Institute of Economic Research Discussion Paper No. 2017, September, 2003), 14.

6. Ibid., 15–16.

7. DiMaggio, Paul J., *Nonprofit Enterprise in the Arts: Studies in Mission and Constraint* (New York: Oxford University Press, 1986), 48.

8. Glaeser, "Reinventing Boston," 16.

9. Sheehan, "Unique to Boston," 3.

10. Dalzell, Robert F., Jr., *Enterprising Elite: The Boston Associates and the World They Made* (Cambridge: Harvard University Press, 1987), 5.

11. Ibid., 5–6.

12. Ibid.

13. Ware, Caroline F., *The Early New England Cotton Manufacture: A Study in Industrial Beginnings* (Boston: Houghton Mifflin Company, 1931), 140–141.

14. Hall, *Why Should Men*, 154.

15. McGouldrick, Paul F., *New England Textiles in the Nineteenth Century: Profits and Investment* (Cambridge: Harvard University Press, 1965), 81.

16. Ibid., 81 and 251 for statistics. Dalzell, *Enterprising Elite*, 52 contains a similar table using McGouldrick's data.

17. White, Gerald T., *A History of the Massachusetts Hospital Life Insurance Company* letter from Lowell to Samuel Appleton dated Dec. 26, 1934 (Cambridge: Harvard University Press, 1955), 200.

18. Laws of Massachusetts, 1818 Chap. 180, Sec. 7.

19. White, *Massachusetts Hospital*, 18.

20. Ibid., 182.

21. Ibid., 9.

22. Dalzell, *Enterprising Elite*, 105-106.

23. Ibid., 106.

24. Farrell, Betty G., *Elite Families: Class and Power in Nineteenth-Century Boston* (Albany: State University of New York Press, 1993), 55.

25. Dalzell, *Enterprising Elite*, 106.

26. Farrell, *Elite Families*, 55.

27. Dalzell, *Enterprising Elite*, 106.

28. Davis, Lance Edwin, "Stock Ownership in the Early New England Textile Industry," *Business History Review*, vol. 32, No. 2 (Summer, 1958), 212.

29. Dalzell, *Enterprising Elite*, 28.
30. Beerman, Kenton, "The Beginning of a Revolution: Waltham and the Boston Manufacturing Company," *The Concord Review, Inc.* (1994), 143.
31. Ibid.
32. Dalzell, *Enterprising Elite*, 28.
33. Ware, *Early New England*, 147.
34. Ibid.
35. Mass. Gen. Laws ch. LIII (1830).
36. *Harvard College v. Amory*, 29 Mass. 446 (1830).
37. Davis, "Stock Ownership," 221.
38. Ibid., 216.
39. Farrell, *Elite Families*, 44.
40. Dalzell, *Enterprising Elite*, 79.
41. Ibid.
42. Ayer, J.C., *Some of the Usages and Abuses in the Management of Our Manufacturing Corporations* (Lowell: C.M. Langley & Co., 1863), 16.
43. "City of Boston," 36.
44. Hall, Peter Dobkin, "What the Merchants Did With Their Money: Charitable and Testamentary Trusts in Massachusetts, 1780–1880," in *Entrepreneurs: The Boston Business Community 1700–1850*, Wright, Conrad Edick and Viens, Katheryn P., eds. (Massachusetts Historical Society, 1997), 377.
45. Friedman, Lawrence M., "The Dynastic Trust," *Yale Law Journal* vol. 73 (March, 1964), 554–555.
46. A popular pamphlet published in 1846 listed Bostonians "credibly" reported to be worth more than $100,000 with brief biographical sketches. See, *Our First Men*.
47. Curtis, Caroline Gardiner, *Memories of Fifty Years in the Last Century* (Boston: Privately Printed, 1947), 11–12.
48. Pessen, Edward, Riches, *Class and Power Before the Civil War* (Lexington: D.C. Heath, 1973), 215.
49. Ibid.

The Beneficiary: Control and Care

1. Haskins, George L., "The Beginnings of Partible Inheritance in the American Colonies," *Yale Law Journal*, vol. 51 (1941–1942), quoting Mass. Col. Laws 1660–1672 (1889), 1282.
2. Beckert, Jens, *Inherited Wealth* (Princeton: Princeton University Press, 2008), 174.
3. Ibid., 184.
4. Haskins, *Partible Inheritance*, 1298.
5. Ibid., 1295, fn 125.
6. Ibid., 1295.
7. Ibid., 1281.

8. Holmes, *Elsie Venner*, 2.

9. White, *Massachusetts Hospital*, 13.

The Law

1. *Barrell v. Joy*, 16 Mass. 221, 228–229 (1819).

2. Curren, William J., "The Struggle for Equity Jurisdiction in Massachusetts," *Boston University Law Review*, vol. 31 (1951), 276.

3. *Black v. Black*, 4 Pick. 234 (1826); *Bridgen v. Cheever*, 10 Mass. 450 (1813).

4. *Prescott v. Tarbell*, 1 Mass. 204, 208 (1804).

5. See Curren, *Equity Jurisdiction*, for a full discussion of Story's involvement.

6. STAT. 1817 c. 87.

7. Peter Dobkin Hall's excellent series of articles and papers on the Boston Brahmins identifies many of these concepts. Particularly, see, Hall, "What Merchants Did with Their Money."

8. *Nightingale v. Burrell*, 32 Mass. 104, 111 (1833).

9. Waggoner, Lawrence W., "From Here to Eternity: The Folly of Perpetual Trusts," *University of Michigan Law School Public Law and Legal Theory Research Series*, (September, 2012), 7.

10. "City of Boston," 36.

11. 133 Mass. 170 (1882).

12. Griswold, Erwin Nathaniel, *Spendthrift Trusts; Restraints on the Alienation of Equitable Interests Imposed by the Terms of the Trust or by Statute* Albany: M. Bender & Co., 1936. Reprinted General Books, 2009, 161.

13. *Braman v. Stiles*, 19 Mass. 460, 464 (1824).

14. Ibid.

15. *Russell v. Lewis*, 19 Mass. 507, 512 (1824).

16. 69 Mass. 405 (1855).

17. Review of *Commentaries on the Law of Trusts and Trustees as Administered in England and in the United States of America* by Charles Fisk Beach (1897), *Law Quarterly Review*, vol 55 (1898), 323.

18. *Barrell v. Joy*, 16 Mass. 221, 228–229 (1819).

19. Stebbings, *The Private Trustee*, 35.

20. Gruff, Jules, "Compensation of Trustees in New York," *New York University Law Review*, vol. 33 (1958), 51.

21. *Barrell v. Joy*, 16 Mass. 221, 229 (1819).

22. "City of Boston," 36.

23. Rounds, Charles E. Jr., and Rounds, Charles E. III, *Loring: A Trustee's Handbook* (Austin: Aspen Publishers, 2009), 773.

24. White, *Massachusetts Hospital* (Appendix 2: Proposals of the Massachusetts Life Insurance Company), 178.

25. Dalzell, *Enterprising Elite*, fn 50, p. 257–258.

Notes

26. 99 Mass. 101 (1868).

27. *Minot v. Paine*, 99 Mass. 101, 112 (1868).

28. Sargent, John Osborne, *A Third Chapter on The Rule in Minot's Case* (G.P. Putnam's Sons, 1874), 4.

29. Sargent, John Osborne, *Common Sense versus Judicial Legislation* (New York: G.P. Putnam and Sons, 1871), 5–6.

30. 149 Mass. 454 (1889).

31. *Claflin v. Claflin*, 149 Mass. 19, 22–23 (1889).

Trust Investments

1. Bowditch, N. I., *A History of the Massachusetts General Hospital* Second Edition Boston: Trustees of the Bowditch Fund, 1872, Reprint Edition (New York: Arno Press, 1872), 66.

2. Will of John McLean, 3.

3. Letter from Francis and Jonathan Amory to "the Committee on the part of Harvard and of M. G. Hospital" dated December 13, 1823, Judicial Archives, Massachusetts Archives, Boston, Massachusetts.

4. The Act establishing probate courts in each county made the Supreme Judicial Court the Supreme Court of Probate. STAT. 1783 c. 40 §31.

5. 29 Mass. 446 (1830).

6. See generally, *The Historical Collections of the Danvers Historical Society*, vol. 10 (Danvers: Danvers Historical Society, 1922): 1–42.

7. Bartol, C.A., *A Discourse on the Life and Character of Samuel Putnam, LL.D., A.A.S., Late Judge of the Supreme Judicial Court of Massachusetts, Delivered in the West Church* (Boston: Crosby, Nichols, and Company, 1853), 6.

8. Ibid., 7.

9. Putnam, Samuel, "Letter to N. I. Bowditch from Samuel Putnam, November 17, 1851" (1851). Bowditch, N. I., *Letters Received 1848–1861*. Collection of the Boston Athenæum, Boston, Massachusetts.

10. *Massachusetts General Hospital v. Amory*, 19 Pick. 445 (1832).

11. Farrell, *Elite Families*, 122.

12. Reno, *The Judiciary*, 502.

13. White *Massachusetts Hospital*, 25.

14. Reno, *The Judiciary*, 503.

15. See, Putnam, Samuel, "Letter to Lemuel Shaw from Samuel Putnam, January 28, 1842" (1842). *The Correspondence of Lemuel Shaw*. Paper 6. http://lawdigitalcommons.bc.edu/rbr_shaw/6.

16. 3 Atk. 441 (1746).

17. *Harvard College v. Amory*, 29 Mass. 446, 459 (1830).

18. Perry, Jairus Ware, *A Treatise on the Law of Trusts and Trustees*, vol. I 3rd edition (Cambridge: University Press, 1882), 564.

19. *Harvard College v. Amory*, 462–463.

20. 29 Mass. 446, 461 (1830).
21. See Shattuck, Mayo Adams, *An Estate Planners Handbook* (Boston: Little, Brown and Company, 1948) (Appendix A to Chapter VI) for a phrase by phrase analysis of Putnam's famous paragraph.
22. *King v. Talbot,* 40 N.Y. 76, 85–86 (1869).
23. Ibid., 86.
24. Ibid., 88.
25. Friedman, "The Dynastic Trust," 566.
26. 3 Atk. 441 (1746).
27. For a comparison of the two jurisdiction's approaches, See, Robson, J. L., "Investment of Trust Funds in Massachusetts and Pennsylvania," *Journal of Comparative Legislation and International Law*, Third Series, vol. 21, No. 4 (1939): 205–219.
28. Act of March 29, 1832, No. 99, P.L. 190 § XIV.
29. *Hemphill's Appeal*, 18 Pa. 303, 308–309 (1852).
30. *Harvard College v. Amory*, 461.
31. PA Const. Art. 3, § 22 (1874).
32. 1 Md. General Laws (Scott & M'Cullough 1869), Art. 93 § 237, at 670.
33. Friedman, "The Dynastic Trust," 563.
34. Loring, Augustus, P., *A Trustee's Handbook* (Boston: Little, Brown, and Company, 1898), 98.

The Trustee

1. Will of John McLean, 13.
2. National Conference of Commissioners on Uniform State Laws, UNIF. TRUST CODE, § 706 (2005).
3. Ibid.
4. Scott, Austin Wakeman, et al., *Scott and Asher on Trusts* §11.1.6.4. 5th ed. (New York: Aspen Publishers, 2006).
5. *Meinhard v. Salmon*, 249 N.Y. 458, 464 (1928).

Massachusetts Lawyer Trustees

1. Holbrook, *The Boston Trustee*, 13.
2. Sheehan, "Unique to Boston," 3.
3. Curren, *Equity Jurisdiction*, 273.
4. Restatement (Second) of Trusts 171 cmt. h (1959).
5. For modern discussions of the ethical issues raised by lawyers drafting documents in which they are named as trustees, see, "ABA Report of the Special Study Committee on Professional Responsibility: Preparation of Wills and Trusts that Name Drafting Lawyer as Fiduciary," 28 *Real Property, Probate and Trust Journal* 803–824 (Winter, 1994) and *ACTEC: Commentaries on the Model Rules of Professional Conduct* (Fourth ed.) (2006).
6. ABA Formal Ethics Opinion 02–426 (May 31, 2002).

Notes

7. Cal. Prob. Code §10804; N.J. Ethics Op. 683 (1996); Georgia Formal Advisory Opinion No. 91-1 (Sept. 13, 1991).
8. Mass. Gen. Laws ch. 203E, §1008 (2012).
9. Altman, James M., "Considering the A.B.A's 1908 Canons of Ethics," 71 *Fordham Law Review* 2395 (2003).
10. deFuria, Joseph W. Jr., "A Matter of Ethics Ignored: The Attorney-Draftsman as Testamentary Fiduciary," 36 *Kansas Law Review* (1987–1988), 275.
11. *Blake v. Pegram*, 109 Mass. 541, 553 (1872).

Competitive Landscape

1. White, *Massachusetts Hospital*, 60.
2. *Trustees of Phillips Academy v. King*, 12 Mass. 546 (1816).
3. Adams, *Boston Money Tree*, 224.
4. See Smith, James. G., *The Development of Trust Companies in the United States* (New York: Henry Holt and Company, 1928), 227–282.
5. Friedman, "The Dynastic Trust," 548.
6. White, *Massachusetts Hospital* (Appendix 2: Proposals of the Massachusetts Life Insurance Company), 182.
7. Farrell, *Elite Families*, 52.
8. White, *Massachusetts Hospital*, 38–39.
9. Ibid., 206.
10. Ibid., 34.
11. Ibid., 41.
12. Ibid., 37.
13. Bowditch, *Mécanique Céleste*, 90.
14. Lehman, "Prudent Man's Last Stand," 31.
15. Ibid.
16. Ibid., 82.
17. Ibid., 33.
18. Ibid., 83.
19. Friedman, "The Dynastic Trust," 563.
20. Laws of the State of New York, 45th Session 1822, ch 50.
21. Lanier, Henry Wysham, *Banking in New York 1822–1922* (New York: The Gillis Press, 1922), 280.
22. Smith, *Trust Companies*, 257–258.
23. *Charter of Morris Canal and Banking Company and the Several Acts of the Legislature in Relation thereto* (Jersey City: Bergen Courier, 1832), 19.
24. Barnes, Andrew Wallace, *History of the Philadelphia Stock Exchange, Banks and Banking* (Philadelphia: Cornelius Baker, Inc., 1911), 21.
25. Smith, *Trust Companies*, 317.
26. Ibid., 305.
27. Ibid.

Individual and Corporate Trustees: A Comparison

1. "Boston Special Correspondence: Professional Trusteeship and Trust Companies of New England," *Trust Companies Magazine*, May 1908 vol. VI, No. 5, 318.
2. Old Colony Trust Company, *The Management of Trust Property* (1904), 3.
3. White *Massachusetts Hospital* (Appendix 2: Proposals of the Massachusetts Life Insurance Company), 178.
4. "Boston Special Correspondence," 318.
5. Ibid.
6. Ibid.
7. Restatement (Second) of Trusts § 171 (1958).
8. Scott, *Scott and Asher on Trusts*, 1173.
9. Uniform Trust Code § 807 cmt. re delegation by trustees.
10. Mass. Gen. Laws ch. 203E, § 807 (2012).
11. Holbrook, *The Boston Trustee*, 16.
12. *New England Merchants National Bank v. Centenary Methodist Church et al.*, 342 Mass. 360 (1961).
13. Welch, E. Sohier, "The Professional Trustee," *Trust Companies Magazine*, Aug., 1936, 174.
14. *In the Matter of Augustus P. Loring, Jr.*, 11 S.E.C. 885 (July 20, 1942).
15. Rule 202(a)(11)(G)-1 [17 CFR 275.202(a)(11)(G)-1].
16. Pub. L. No. 111-203, 124 Stat. 1376.
17. Smith, *Trust Companies*, 75.
18. Kirkbride, F. B. and Sterrett, J. E., *The Modern Trust Company, its Functions and Organization* (New York: The Macmillan Company, 1905), 5 quoting from "Trust and Title Insurance Companies," *Lippincott's Magazine*, Vol. XLII 88.

The Franklin Fund

1. McCleary, Samuel F., *A Sketch of the Origin, Object and Character of the Franklin Fund, For the Benefit of Young Married Mechanics of Boston* (Boston: Alfred Mudge & Son, 1866), 10.
2. Ibid., 36.
3. Van Doren, Carl, *Benjamin Franklin* (New York, The Viking Press, 1938), 763.
4. McCleary, *Franklin Fund*, 12.
5. Ibid., 35.
6. White, *Massachusetts Hospital*, 40.
7. McCleary, *Franklin Fund*, 27.
8. Ibid., 28.
9. Ibid., 37.

Notes

10. Baltzell, E. Digby, *Puritan Boston and Quaker Philadelphia: two Protestant ethics and the spirit of class authority and leadership* (New York: Free Press, 1979), 208.
11. "From Ben Franklin, a Gift That's Worth Two Fights," *New York Times* April 21, 1990.
12. Baltzell, *Puritan Boston*, 208.
13. Lehman, "Prudent Man's Last Stand," 33.

Codicil

1. Paul Harvey's catch line for his series of shows with surprising endings.
2. Ibid., 67.
3. Ibid., 64 and 727.
4. Bowditch, *Massachusetts General*, 73.
5. Ibid., 77.
6. Boylan, Anne M., *The Origins of Women's Activism: New York and Boston, 1797–1840* (Chapel Hill: University of North Carolina Press, 2002), 66–67.
7. Trust under declaration of John Lowell, John Amory Lowell and Rufus G. Lowell fbo Ann McLean dated August 14, 1829. Judicial Archives, Massachusetts Archives, Boston, Massachusetts.
8. Lee, William, *John Leigh of Agawam (Ipswich) Massachusetts 1634–1671 and His Descendants of the Name of Lee* (Albany: Joel Munsell's Sons, 1888), 266.
9. Lee, William, *A Yankee Jeffersonian: Selections from the Diary and Letters of William Lee of Massachusetts*, Written from 1796 to 1840, edited by Mary Lee Mann (Cambridge: The Belknap Press, 1958), 239.
10. Ibid.
11. Ibid., 268.
12. Ibid., 240–241.

Current Boston Trustees

1. "What Do These Two Have in Common: They Use Their Lawyers as Money Managers," *The Boston Globe* November 2, 2000, C1.
2. Curtis, Charles P., "Manners and Customs," 41.

Conclusion

1. Greenslet, Ferris, *The Lowells and Their Seven Worlds* (Boston: Houghton Mifflin Co., 1946), 322.
2. Welch, "The Professional Trustee," 175.

Selected Bibliography

Boston Brahmins and Society:

Dalzell, Robert F., Jr., *Enterprising Elite: The Boston Associates and the World They Made* (Cambridge: Harvard University Press, 1987)

Farrell, Betty G., *Elite Families: Class and Power in Nineteenth-Century Boston* (Albany: State University of New York Press, 1993)

Glaeser, Edward L., *Reinventing Boston: 1640–2003,* Harvard Institute of Economic Research (Preliminary Draft, Sept. 9, 2003)

White, Gerald T., *A History of the Massachusetts Hospital Life Insurance Company* (Cambridge: Harvard University Press, 1955)

Boston Trustees:

"City of Boston," *Fortune,* Vol. VII, No. 2 (Feb. 1933): 26–106

Curtis, Charles P., "Manners and Customs of the Boston Trustee," 1958 *A.B.A. Sec. Real Prop. Prob. & Tr. Proc.* (1958): 40–43

Hall, Peter Dobkin, "What the Merchants Did with Their Money: Charitable and Testamentary Trusts in Massachusetts, 1780-1880," in *Entrepreneurs: The Boston Business Community 1700–1850*, eds. Conrad Edick Wright and Katheryn P. Viens (Massachusetts Historical Society, 1997): 365–421

Hall, Peter Dobkin and George E. Marcus, "Why Should Men Leave Great Fortunes to Their Children?," in *Inheritance and Wealth in America*, ed. Robert K. Miller and Stephen J. McNamee (New York: Plenham Press, 1998) 139–171

Holbrook, Donald, *The Boston Trustee* (Boston: Marshall Jones Company, 1937)

Lehman, Milton, "The Prudent Man's Last Stand," *Nation's Business* (March 1949): 31–83

Selected Bibliography

Sheehan, William J., "Unique to Boston are the Famous 'Boston Trustees,'" *Boston Evening Transcript*, July 28, 1934

Welch, E. Sohier, "The Professional Trustee," *Trust Companies Magazine*, (August, 1936): 173–180

NATHANIEL BOWDITCH:

Loring, Augustus P., Jr., *Nathaniel Bowditch (1773–1838) of Salem and Boston Navigator, etc.* (New York: Newcomen Society, 1950)

TEXTILE INDUSTRY:

Beerman, Kenton, "The Beginning of a Revolution: Waltham and the Boston Manufacturing Company," *The Concord Review, Inc.* (1994): 141–157

Davis, Lance Edwin, "Stock Ownership in the Early New England Textile Industry," *Business History Review*, vol. 32, No. 2 (Summer, 1958): 204–222

McGouldrick, Paul F., *New England Textiles in the Nineteenth Century: Profits and Investment* (Cambridge: Harvard University Press, 1965)

TRUSTS, TRUSTEES, AND THE LAW:

Curran, William J., "The Struggle for Equity Jurisdiction in Massachusetts," *Boston University Law Review*, Vol. 31 (1951): 269–296

Friedman, Lawrence M., "The Dynastic Trust," *Yale Law Journal* Vol. 73 (March 1964): 547–592

Loring, Augustus P., *A Trustee's Handbook* (Boston: Little, Brown, and Company, 1898)

Smith, James G., *The Development of Trust Companies in the United States* (New York: Henry Holt and Company, 1928)

Index

Index

Index

Practical Navigator, The (Moore), 41
Pratt, Harold I. "Harry," 9–10, 136
Prescott v. Tarbell, 71, 154
primogeniture, 67
private trustees, 35, 119–120
professional trustees, 13, 30–48, 72, 81, 96–99
Provident Institution for Savings, 129
Provisional Congress, 18
Prudent Man Rule, 10, 32, 42, 72, 85, 86, 89–90
Puritans, 67, 71
Putnam, Samuel, 72, 85–87, 88–89, 94
Putnam, Samuel R., 87

Quincy, Josiah, 18, 51
Quincy, Josiah, Jr., 38

Rackemann, Sawyer & Brewster, 136
Restatement of Trusts, 1992, 102
Revolutionary War, 18, 20, 64
Rice, Heard & Bigelow, Inc., 39, 136
Ropes & Gray, LLP, 136
Ropes & Ward, 44
Rugo v. Rugo, 25, 149
Rule Against Perpetuities, 72–74, 81
Rule in Minot's Case, 79–80
Russell v. Lewis, 75–76

Saltonstall & Co., 135
Securities and Exchange Commission (SEC), 123–124
Sewall, Samuel, 86
Shaw, Lemuel, 73, 88
shipping and maritime industry
American navigation, 41–42
economic growth in, 52, 53, 61
registered tonnage, 53
supercargoes, 41–42, 44
Sohier, Edward Dexter, 36, 44–45, 136
South Sea Company, 88
Spendthrift Clause, 73, 74–76
State Street, 62
State Street Safe Deposit & Trust Company, 112
Story, Joseph, 72
Stuart, Gilbert, 131

Index

COLOPHON

The book is set entirely in Miller, a transitional typeface designed by Matthew Carter in 1997 and based
on the sturdy Scotch models designed by Richard
Austin in the early nineteenth century. Scotch was
a popular typeface in Boston, and would have been
an appropriate choice for law and trust documents.
Miller was initially designed for the *Boston Globe*,
and features automatic nonaligning figures. This
book was designed and typeset by Sara Eisenman.